Acknowledgment

For Rory, Ajuré and Bria

The true loves of my life

Don't let anyone else's opinions stop you from achieving your goals.

REALITY CHECK

Does Race Define a Relationship?

By Valerie C. Eaton

© Copyright October 2010 Valerie C. Eaton

Cover by Bria Waterman

Table of Contents

Lisa

RRRING!! "Damn. I knew I should have taken the day off from work." Lisa looked at the gaudy, rhinestone-lacquered alarm clock and hated her ex-husband even more for giving it to her. She thought it was cute when he gave it to her for their second anniversary.

Tom had forgotten about their anniversary and was reminded when Lisa gave him a gift. He ran out mumbling something about needing a pack of cigarettes returning with her less-than-thoughtful gift from the corner Hallmark store.

"Mark! Get up! You'll be late to school." "Way ahead of you, Mom!" He replied to his mother while peeking his head into her art-deco bedroom. He looked at his mother's dark chocolate complexion and perfectly permed hair. He subconsciously felt glad his father was white, attributing to his mulatto racial designation. Lisa looked at her fair skinned, strait-haired son with the thought that he was the one good thing that came out of her 20-year mixed marriage.

Tom

"Umph." Tom sat up in the lumpy mattress and looked over at his latest meaningless one-night stand lying beside him. This one was just as boring (in bed) as the others, but she was black. When he picked her up in the nightclub the night before, his first thought was of Lisa and how great she was in bed.

Tom recalled meeting Lisa for the first time.

"Would you like to dance?" He asked over the music at the trendy night club. The club catered to a mixed crowd. Tonight was a predominantly black crowd. Tom liked nights like this at the club. The DJ usually played according to the majority. An old favorite of Lisa's was playing and Tom had heard it so often, it was one of his favorites as well. As Cheryl Lynn and the crowd screamed the lyrics..."To be Real..." the young black college student replied, "sure?" They danced provocatively all night to every R&B hit on the charts. He had decided he would ask her to come "for a ride." He found his opportunity during a D'Angelo remake of a song he couldn't recall but remembered it was D'Angelo since all the women usually swooned as he belted out something about brown sugar or how IT made them feel... Lisa had once told him that D'Angelo will make any black woman wet her pants. That advice came in handy. Tom wasn't even aware of her name just as much as he didn't remember the record playing. She didn't even bat an eye when the so called "ride" ended in front of the nearest motel. In order not to sound too presumptuous, he asked, "You sure you want to go for THIS ride?" She replied, "I got in the car, didn't I?" Tom was a little taken aback by her forwardness. His latest conquests were lonely homemakers and recent divorcees. Her forwardness carried over into the bed. He was used to being the aggressor and it clearly wasn't the case with her. She put his hands where she wanted them, told him when, how fast, how far in and when to come. He complied. Though not the norm, Tom liked it but paid for it later.

Lisa had been his first. First black woman. The whole idea of having a black woman dazzled him so much that marriage seemed like the right thing to do at the time. The lovemaking was so unbelievable that the production of a child was inevitable.

Tom and Lisa often ate out for dinner at baseball games, at concerts or at restaurants. The dinner was always seafood (as they both believed in "natural" aphrodisiacs). They always ate quietly gazing sensually into each other's eyes while eating suggestively. Every meal ended in sex. Most times, not waiting until they got home. Tom once "fingered" Lisa under the table at one of the finest restaurants in town. Lisa came with an exhausted gasp gaining the attention of nearby tables. Lisa never went to the restaurant again. She was not, in Tom's mind, a spontaneous woman but she was certainly "down for whatever." One not-so-normal night as they lie sweaty and exhausted, Lisa had her hand on her stomach. Tom joked and said, "I hope I didn't hurt the baby." Lisa looked Tom straight in the eye and said, "No, you didn't." Tom spoke with his eyes and asked her to confirm. She answered by making love to Tom confirming her undying love to him. Tom was sex-drunk, induced by the excitement over his ability to produce a child.

Tom's friends thought it was a culturally bold statement to have an interracial marriage and Lisa's friends and family members were all sure it would fail (ultimately, they were right). These two factors, on one hand, encouraged their marriage to succeed and, on the other, had made it a marriage of rebellion. Tom was a good-looking middle-aged white man and was always the center of attention. Having a black companion intrigued his friends more than surprised them.

When Tom and Lisa took a break from their incessant sexual encounters, they introduced each other to their respective worlds. Tom and Lisa's first step out of the closet was at a basketball game where they met Tom's Knick-crazed coworkers. They had floor seats, not that it mattered to Lisa who knew nothing about this or any other sport. Tom was in front of Lisa as he approached Bill and Tyrone. Tyrone blurted out, "where's your sex-muffin?" Tom, very insulted by the comment, stepped to the side to reveal Lisa and said, "Guys, this is my fiancée, Lisa. Lisa, the guys." Lisa hadn't heard the comment over all the noise of the basketball game and the fans. She shook both their hands but instinctively didn't like Tyrone. From that moment on, Tyrone was non-existent, not only to Lisa, but to Tom as well. It only took the "guys" one day to spread the word of Tom's new black fiancé to the rest of the office.

As the pain of a bad back, emphasized by cheap hotel beds, set in, he thought aloud mumbling, "I'm getting too old to keep this up much longer." He patted the young conquest on the butt to wake her as he realized his buddy (and coworker) Bill should be pulling up any minute to pick him up. Instinctively, the young woman rolled out of bed with the sheet wrapped around her and headed for the bathroom. Tom yelled out, "Not too long in there, okay?" In 5 minutes, the woman was dressed. She looked at Tom, rolled her eyes and told him she'd call him later. This was, as Tom knew it, another way of saying thanks, but it was just a night ...got too drunk and now I regret it.

As Bill pulled up to Tom's posh apartment building (doorman and all), Tom could barely get in the passenger seat before Bill started the inquisition. Mondays were the highlight of Bill, his middle-aged, twice-married, business partner's life who listened intently to Tom's weekend adventures. "Well, how many?" Tom looked at his colleague and thought to lie, but didn't. "One." "What kind?" "Bla...African American." "Ooo, excuse me. I thought you said Lisa was the last." Bill had already driven at least 4 blocks taking yellow lights at each corner. "I know, but this was different somehow. Bill?" "Yeah Tom." "No details today, ok?" As Bill silently applauded himself for catching the lights, he continued to prod. "Come on Tom, you know I only survive the weekends with Marge knowing your stories are coming Monday mornings. They revive the life in me." "I know, but I.... WATCH IT! Tom Yelled. Bill's car had just missed a bunch of school children and went smack into a parked car flipping over and hitting a stone wall. Bill died never hearing one of Tom's weekend tales. A tradition for the past 10 years. 9 of which were when he was still with Lisa.

Lisa Meets Marge

Lisa was half dressed and in the middle of brushing her teeth when the phone rang. "Hello ..... Yes." Lisa didn't recognize the strained voice on the other end of the phone. She would not have recognized Marge's voice right away anyhow. Lisa had only met her a few times at office parties and "picnics" Tom's job had sponsored. Lisa was always told that picnic was short for what the southern lynch mobs used for "pick a nigger" and gave Tom this knowledge when he initially invited her to one of them. He was appalled and insisted it wasn't true. This was one of their first arguments that were racially motivated.

There was a lump in Lisa's throat the size of an apple when Marge revealed the news. Tom was in ICU and unconscious. Lisa gave her condolences to Marge and asked the details. She immediately looked for Mark's class schedules. Not only did she want him to know about what happened but she needed his comfort as well.

Mark looked at his phone as it rang and wondered who could be calling him at school. He had an eerie feeling before answering the call from his mother. He sensed the distress and tried to calm his mother down while listening to what had happened to his father. Even though his mother had been the strongest and most dependable parent, she never dealt with emotional situations well.

When Lisa arrived at the hospital, Mark at her side, the only thing she could think of was the fact that Mark was born there. Marge and her daughter Susan were exiting in tears as Lisa and Mark approached the hospital doors. Marge knew Lisa right away (being the subject of gossip makes you more memorable). Marge instinctively approached Lisa with open arms. Marge reassured Lisa that Tom would be alright (Lisa wished she could return the sentiment). For some reason Lisa felt compelled to tell Marge that she and Tom had separated months ago (almost a year) but decided against it. After all pleasantries were made and said, Lisa pushed herself to enter the hospital doors and expect the unexpected. Mark was feeling hopeful about his father and at the same time he couldn't help wondering whether or not this girl, Marge's daughter, was involved in a relationship.

Lisa and Mark asked the front desk where Tom's room was and headed to the 4th floor. They entered a room shared with another car accident victim who wasn't as fortunate as Tom and was in a complete body cast. Tom looked over at Lisa and Mark and smiled with gladness that he was not alone. Lisa held the right hand and Mark held the left. Tom explained that he was just banged up but mostly feeling the loss of Bill more than anything. Lisa tried to soothe Tom and convince him to get some rest before asking a nearby doctor what the prognosis was on Tom. The doctor expressed his shock to Lisa to see that Tom had only sustained a concussion and a few broken bones and that he would be back to normal in only a few months.

As Lisa and Mark left the hospital, Lisa was surprised to feel something from Tom. It was a feeling of reconciliation. After a couple of days of going back and forth to the hospital and starting to feel close to Tom again, Lisa received the death announcement for Bill's funeral in the mail. She felt obligated to pay her respects (not to mention the fact that Tom asked her to go because he felt like someone should represent him since he was unable to attend). As Lisa stood amongst the mourners at Bill's funeral, she felt uneasiness. The kind of uneasiness when someone is staring right through you. She tried to use her peripheral vision to see who was giving her this more-than-uncomfortable feeling. She saw one of the women Tom was supposed to have had an affair with. Lisa had a friend who had a friend who worked at Tom's office and often got all the scoops on Tom when she suspected his libido needed a little bit more excitement than she could give him at the time. She didn't have to turn her head very far in the other direction to see another of Tom's "catches of the day" standing at the other side of what seemed to be "co workers of the deceased" corner. When Lisa received the death announcement in the mail, she assumed she was expected at the funeral being that Tom and Bill were best friends. In order not to disappoint Marge (or Tom), Lisa put on her best funeral dress and set out to what would be the start of a strange day. When Lisa realized most eyes were on her she felt anxious for the farewell ceremony to be over. She waited for everyone to start walking up to see the "last remains" and flew to the bathroom as soon as she thought everyone was thinking about how well the morticians prepared the body. When she entered the ladies room, there was another black woman standing in front of the mirror. She was putting on powdered foundation (Lisa thought, "Who puts that goop on anymore?"). "Hi, my name is Velma." "Hi," Lisa said. "Don't worry, honey, they just wonderin' who you are." Lisa replied in her mind...*Well.... excuse me, do I know you (and who the hell you calling honey?).* Velma answered as if she heard Lisa's thoughts. "I was Bill's secretary, I saw you at the company picnic some years ago." *Ugh, there goes that word again*, she thought. Lisa really didn't care where she had seen her but nonetheless answered in order to seem sociable. "Oh. Well, I don't know if anyone knows, but Tom and Bill were in the accident together." "Oh yeah, they know. They also know that you and Tom split up. They think it's because you found out about, well, you know." "Well, *(as if it's any of your damn business but I'll tell you in a nice way because we have a*

sisterhood that cannot be replaced, she thought sarcastically)
I came here out of respect for the fact that Bill and Tom were
good friends and I met Marge a couple of times previously."
Velma went on as if not ever hearing a word Lisa said. Don't
get me wrong, honey, (*there she goes with that honey stuff
again*), I don't want to know why…they do. I just had to come
in here and freshen up and get away from those folks (rubbing
one hand on the back of the other indicating she was talking
about white folk). I get enough of this at the office. There's
not a whole lot of us you know." Not that that made Lisa any
more uncomfortable than this woman had made her feel but
Lisa shook her head in understanding anyway. The thought
flashed through Lisa's mind just then that she'd wished Tom
was here with her to ease the tension (he was good at that).
Meanwhile, Tom was still in the hospital wishing he were
dead (from all the pain he was in). Lisa, again, paid her
condolences to Marge and her family and gave the old "If
there's anything I can do…" speech. She left, went home, and
opened the mail she had picked up from Tom's house. It had
been a week and a half before the accident since Tom had
actually sat home long enough to do

the mail himself. There was one solicitation postcard that particularly struck her eye. Tom always threw these things in the garbage and chastised her for always buying products advertised by any unknown company in the world. Lisa had spent a small fortune on these items, but Tom always seemed to find a way to use every one. It was an advertisement for a dream analysis book. She put it on the shelf next to the television to remind herself to send for it.

Back Together?

When Tom was discharged from the hospital, Lisa was there to pick him up (she knew his family was still not over him marrying her and wouldn't be there to pick him up). He had asked her in his most pathetic, begging tone of voice. As they left the hospital, she had an odd feeling, a good feeling. Usually when she was with Tom, she subconsciously expected dirty looks from both black and white people. Today was different. There were no whispers, no second glances and no derogatory remarks about her being his maid, nothing. Tom seemed to be in a daze. He hadn't quite mourned over the loss of his best friend (he hadn't realized Bill was his only real male friend until his untimely death). Though brief, his retrospection was interrupted by the familiar smell of Lisa's perfume and her soft touch on his elbow as she escorted him out of the hospital. Lisa wore the perfume on purpose.

She had dressed that morning having flashbacks with every touch of her body. She stepped in the shower remembering how she invited him in. The stall was too small but they found several positions that worked while exploring each other's body. She stepped out of the shower and looked at her newly polished toes and flash backed to Tom gently rubbing her toes and caressing her leg as he delicately kissed each toe. He then started sucking her big toe and to her surprise, it excited her. She laughed to herself at first but quickly changed the emotion as he reached up to the inner part of her thigh... still sucking her toe. Then she dried herself and as she viewed her pouched stomach, she thought back to Tom making fun of her "teddy bear" belly. She pouted and he apologized by kissing her pouch and telling her how much it turned him on. He kissed it and slowly went further down to kiss and lick. Between all kisses and licking, he told her how wonderfully rounded she was. As she put her bra on, she remembered him telling her how absolutely perfect her breasts were. Just looking at her dressing turned him on. She often went to work late because of their early morning escapades.

Tom had suffered a broken leg, some cracked ribs, a concussion and several scrapes and bruises. His son, Mark, was on his left, aiding in his dismissal from the hospital which was his home for two weeks and three days. Getting in her Toyota, Lisa knew where she wanted to go, but she thought it best to ask, "where to?" Tom assumed she would take him home but the question gave possibilities. Nevertheless, he answered cautiously. "I guess I should go to my place and make sure the mail and telephone messages get taken care of." Tom said this hoping she'd object and take him to her place. Tom had become the typical bachelor. There were dishes stacked in the sink and God knows how many pair of dirty underwear were lying around from his mad dashes to and from his sexual adventures. "I took care of your mail, don't worry, I only separated your bills by priority...those stamped final notice on top." It's not that he couldn't pay them, but he never had time lately to sit down and write and mail the checks. Lisa wanted desperately to have Tom in her bed to hold and nurture back to good health. "Thanks, babe." Well I guess we can go to your place, if you don't mind." Lisa was pleased. The sound of him calling her "babe" again sent a shiver down her spine. "No, I don't mind." Tom smiled inwardly. He knew Lisa felt anger towards him about, well, everything. The only thing good between them was sex. He couldn't even imagine that even after almost a year Lisa had sex with anyone. She was too picky for that (despite their first encounter). He only hoped that her vulnerability got them in bed.

Tom knew his stay at Lisa's would lead to sharing the same bed and the thought of them making love (if that's what you'd call what they did) gave him an erection. Their sexual sessions were always a new adventure and Tom was already thinking of ways to maneuver around his-broken leg and other handicaps. Lisa was thinking the same (although she had no intention of starting anything, Lisa had to make sure that when this interlude was over, and it would be over, it wouldn't be said that she made the first move (even though she did by agreeing to have Tom stay with her during his recuperation)). Lisa hadn't had-sex in the eight months they'd been separated. She remembered the last time Tom had used his magical abilities to get her in bed for a good bye-screw (afterwards, when he said "I bet you'll miss that," she just felt used). Tom had started an argument about Lisa being the one who had destroyed their marriage (Tom knew their arguments always ended in the bed). He had moved the argument from one room to the other ending in the bedroom. While Tom and Lisa pondered over how they were going to handle this recuperation period, Mark had only one thing on his mind. He had to find out how to get in touch with Bill's daughter, Susan.

Mark

Mark knew he was a prime catch for any woman. Except a "down to the bone" black woman. In his opinion, black woman couldn't deal with the fact that he was mulatto and chose to associate more with his "European" side. He had once tried to get "cultural" and connect with his African American sisters and brothers and ended up feeling like he was pretending to be something he wasn't. The sisters and brothers felt that way also. Mark never used slang and didn't really care to. During most conversations, Mark kept quiet and no one knew why. It was because Mark didn't have one clue as to what they were talking about. He tried to date a black girl once when he was 17 and she dumped him calling him an Oreo cookie and a "wanna be." Mark knew she had friends who teased her for seeing him, but he didn't care. He wanted a way out of the relationship anyway because he felt she was only using him to lose her virginity like all the other girls in her group did to unsuspecting good looking boys. Mark was a virgin until he went to college and got laid by a white girl. After the freshman dance, she was so high and spaced out that she had come to his room to see his roommate and (later said) thought Mark was him. The next thing he knew, she was licking his chest calling him a black Mandingo and asking if "it was really true about black men" while unbuckling his Levi's. That's when he decided that white women were more his cup of tea. While Lisa was walking around to the passenger side of the car after driving up to their building, Mark asked his father if he could get Susan's telephone number. Of course the look on Tom's face was as if to say, that's my boy. His *verbal* reply was "Sure Mark, no problem." He had the proudest grin you ever saw on a father's face. Tom always talked very candidly with his son. Mark always felt his father talked about sex too much. Anyway, Mark knew that if he asked ol' dad any question about a girl or anything to do with the opposite sex, there would be no problem getting an answer.

Marge

When Susan got home from her father's funeral, she looked at her mother in hopelessness. Susan always looked at her mother as if she were an "Edith Bunker." On the other hand, Marge couldn't wait to get on with her life. She let her husband control her for 18 years.

Marge stole her husband from a friend of hers (obviously the word friend used very loosely) 18 years ago when her friend confided in her that her husband was a great disappointment to her after being married for only three months. Marge took one look at Bill and felt that he was a dream come true. She had to have him. Marge was young and vibrant back then, she had no trouble getting any man she wanted. Including Bill. She had slipped him her telephone number one night when she was over for dinner. Bill was game for just about anything back then and called her the next day to find out what he could get out of this sexy 23 year old woman who always flirted right in front of his wife. (Bill always excused himself from the room after such an incident, because she turned him on so much his whole face immediately turned red) Marge had made the first move and invited him to a hotel room for lunch. After three dates, Marge's friend found out Bill was seeing someone and found her quick exit from the failing marriage. Marge knew her friend knew it was she that was seeing Bill, but never mentioned it. The last time Marge saw that woman was at her divorce proceedings one month after she and Bill were exclusive. Nevertheless, Marge had to keep an eye on Bill. She didn't want what happened to her friend happen to her, ever. Marge served Bill's every need. She never didn't know where Bill was. She loved Bill.

Now it was time to go on with her life the way she really wanted to (she had tired of him three years prior to his untimely death). Now was the time for her not to have a man at the center of her attention for 24 hours a day. She had already had a plan. She had to wait at least a week or so for the standard mourning period everyone expected her to go through. Not that she wasn't sad that Bill was gone, but Bill left her very comfortable and there was no need to dwell on sad events. It was time to CHARGE IT! She always remembered this line from a Flintstone episode. Susan was wondering what was going on in her mother's head. She knew her mother had no skills to get a job. Even though her father left them comfortable enough for her mother not to have to work for a while, what was going to happen when the money ran out? Susan was sure her life would go on without a blemish. But she couldn't be so sure about her mother. Little did she know. Well, she thought, I can't be bothered right now. I must find out how to get in touch (more like, conveniently bump into) that yummy specimen of a man, Tom's son, Mark. She had seen him around at the University, but knew he hadn't noticed her. She pretty much kept to herself. No loud crowds. Her only interest was boys. She told her analyst she thought she was a nymphomaniac, but only said that to get a rise out of him (he rose). She loved playing with the male species' heads. In her opinion, there was nothing like getting laid. The best time she ever had was with a black guy.

Susan

It was back in 7th grade. She was not a virgin. There weren't many black students in her school and they stayed in their own crowd. They didn't associate with white people, at all. One year, she had to go to summer school. She was failing math. The teachers had found a new way to get out of work and invented A+ student tutors. Susan figured it would be some geek that she would have to spend her entire summer days with instead of flirting with the muscle guys on Byrith's

Beach down the shore. Most of the tutors were already going home for the weekend and there weren't many left to choose from except for those that really needed the money for the holidays. It turned out to be one of the black students. Who'd have thought? Susan had no idea that any one of these guys had that much to offer, brain wise. As the summer got on, she was bound to do the same, get it on. She had heard that black men had big dicks (her favorite word for penis), but had never seen one. She had to find out for herself. She called the school and asked for Jim (the tutor). She told him that she had sprained her ankle and couldn't make it to class for the next week. She even wrapped her ankle in some gauze to make it look more believable. She convincingly told him how her life depended on passing this class and that she would pay him if he could come to her house this week from 2 to 4 p.m. to tutor her (that was the time her mother went to play bridge with the bridge club). Jim (listening to his father's advice, "never pass up an easy buck," and ignoring his mother's advice, "never get involved with a white girl") told Susan he would do it, but just for her. He arrived at her house at 2:00 p.m. sharp. Books in hand, he proceeded to sit down on the couch. Susan asked if he wouldn't mind studying in her room being that everything was there for the convenience of her sprained ankle. *What harm could that do?*, he thought. When they got up to her room, she sat on her bed. It was a typical princess bedroom. The furniture was white wood. It was equipped with a dresser, mirror, armoire, 2 nightstands, a canopy bed with a white netting on the top and a separate white wood desk. She adorned the room with pink accessories and lots of glitter.

Being the gentleman that he was, he sat at her desk and continued to go on with the lesson from where they left off in school. As Susan undressed herself, Jim was so engrossed with what he was teaching her (and, not to mention, in awe at the size of her room), he hadn't notice her. When Jim looked up, he felt his face burn up (if it was possible for a black person to turn red, he did). He told Susan to please put her clothes back on (subconsciously praying that she didn't). She told him to come over to the bed. He got up and explained to her that this was wrong and that he would lose his honor status if anyone found out (bringing to mind the question of whether or not she was still going to pay him).

Jim was still just a young teenager and was not in control over his libido. Susan saw the rise in his pants and got a little scared but more excited at the same time. She knelt on the bed and pulled the zipper down on his hand-me-down pants. Jim didn't remember if his underwear were clean, so he looked down and did a quick check before the zipper was all the way down. He was okay. He then let all of his inhibitions go. He kissed her as if she were the juiciest piece of cold watermelon on the hottest day of the summer. Susan couldn't control herself either. She came before he even got inside her. That didn't matter. She couldn't get enough. Just as they were both climaxing, they were interrupted.

"SUSAN...OH MY GOD! WHAT IS HE DOING TO YOU?! GET OUT, YOU NIGGER, GET OUT! GET OFF OF MY BABY!" "But mama ... I, we, I mean, he forced me and I..." Jim could not believe his ears. This bitch was now accusing him of rape. Jim, never looking back, grabbed his pants, jumped out of Susan's window onto a nearby tree and fled home as fast as his legs could carry him. Susan never saw Jim again. Nor did she experience a black dick again. Jim told his father the story, and they moved out of town that night. It was a small town and they knew what happened to blacks in small towns when it had anything to do with fooling with one of *their* women. Susan got what she wanted and somehow cooled her mother down. She had convinced her that he talked her into having sex and she was curious but that she wasn't forced. Of course, that meant that it wasn't her fault, but it saved Jim from being hunted down like a dog...unfortunately Jim nor his family were made aware of this. After the explanation from her innocent, albeit, scheming daughter, Marge never told Bill. She subconsciously knew that her daughter was exactly like her. They both had to get what they wanted when it came to men.

Marge saw the look in Susan's eyes when they saw Mark at the hospital. She knew Susan would have him soon. Susan called her friend Michelle (friend only of convenience, she called her when she wanted to find out about a particular man on campus). Michelle knew the reason Susan kept her number. She was just wondering who the new piece of meat was, Mark Handly. Michelle was very resourceful. Mark had been hanging out with a guy named Damian and Damian was the brother of her cousin's best friend. Michelle made some calls and had the number for Susan in one half hour (which was a long time for Michelle, but she didn't really like Susan very much and didn't rush). Susan was very aggressive (a bitch to the executives she would come across in her career) and didn't waste any time calling Mark. "Hello?" "Hello, may I speak to Mark." Lisa was in no mood to be inquisitive, so she never asked who it was. Susan heard Lisa yell for Mark after telling her to hold on. Good, she thought, he's home.

Lisa and Mark

As Lisa handed Mark the phone, her mind wondered back (as if it never left) to Tom. Tom made himself very comfortable. He had already found his way to the bedroom within the two hours they had been home. Lisa had prepared a meal (making sure it was an ordinary one as not to make Tom think she went through any trouble just for him) before picking him up from the hospital. They ate almost as soon as they entered the apartment. Lisa walked into her single-lifestyle bedroom (the one thing great about Tom leaving was the fact that she could adjust the room to her tastes, her styles and most of all, keep it clean), and reassured Tom that he would be sleeping in the guest room tonight (it used to be his smoking, hang-out-and-play-poker room) and advised him not to get too comfortable. "Ah, come on Lis." "Don't even try it" was Lisa's reply even though she *did* want him to try it. Tom switched the subject to Mark. "Who was that?...Someone for Mark?...Some new chick?" "I wish you'd stop referring to women as chicks." "Okay, new babe," "You are hopeless," sighed Lisa. Lisa knew how much Tom admired the fact that Mark was sexually active and had heard him bragging to his friends one night. "I can't afford it, man. I pay for schooling, clothing, and not to mention making sure Mark has an ample supply of rubbers, heh heh ... chip off the old block ya know..." he said one night in a drunken stupor after one of his famous leave-the-house-smelling-like-smoke poker games. These comments bothered Lisa but had also made her glad. Not just for the fact that Mark was having sex, but how the fear of him being homosexual and of him being some kind of yuppie introvert who couldn't muster up enough nerve to speak to a woman, was put to rest. Although those fears should have vanished when he was a toddler who was so engrossed with the female anatomy, she almost feared him being a pervert. Tom couldn't wait to have his monthly catch up session with Mark's sex life (including the chick now on the phone). But that could wait, right now, he was interested in finding out how Lisa's love life was going. On the off chance she was getting some (as he so eloquently had asked her over the phone on one of his get-drunk-because-I-feel-lonely nights. Lisa was the only one who understood how he felt when he was in this mood), he would politely ask who it was and try to "get off" on it while trying to seduce her at the same time. If she wasn't seeing anyone, it would be sinfully easy (he mused) to rectify this problem. As Lisa looked at Tom, with the thought that he was probably thinking about sex, she made a vow to herself ... no matter how horny she gets, he's not getting into her pants..... At least not until the last possible moment when he stops trying. "Hello?" Mark answered the phone. "Hi." Susan replied in her most chipper voice. "You may not remember me, but I'm

Bill's daughter, your father's friend. Well, not that I was your father's friend, but Bill, my father, was." Susan wanted to seem a little nervous though she wasn't. She knew how to play the game all too well. The thought in Mark's mind was exactly what he replied, "Oh yeah (oh yeah, oh yeah)." Mark couldn't believe his luck. It was kismet. He had used that lingo when it was appropriate which always reminded him of the time he dated a "chick" (like father like son) who was into astrology.

Mark

She was a little spaced for Mark, but he was intrigued and fascinated by her knowledge of the stars. He was always amazed at how much she knew about his personality just through reading his astrology chart. She also talked a lot about aura and stuff like that. He was a Libra and she was a Capricorn. This combination was only good for the sex, she had told him once, since he was supposed to be unstable in love affairs, was very "own way" and was not apt to even think about a serious relationship with anyone until he was in the age range of 25 to 35. Mark, being the man he was, could care less what she thought. As a matter of fact, it was even better this way. He didn't have to make up any phony excuses when he got tired of her and he never had to lie about where he was. She had her life and he had his. The sex, of course, was incredible. He found out she had VD and even though she argued that he was fooling around (and he never denied it), he had only been having sex with her. That was the end of that.

Mark and Susan

Susan had continued the conversation with a little more ease in her tone of voice. "So, I've seen you around the University. What's your major?" "Science." Mark replied. Mark had known he wanted to be a biochemist since he was a junior in High School (an early career decision, he reasoned this was an attribute of a Libra and should follow this path). It was around that time he found out about his great-aunt going into a deep depression. He had asked his science teacher (his mentor of 2 years) what had caused depression and was told about the change in a person's biochemistry due to a saddening event in their life and how it could cause a psychological depression. "That's why there are scientists such as biochemists to figure out balances of the nature in a living organism." His mentor had finished explaining, sounding like the guy on the career orientation video Mark saw when he first entered college. Science? Susan thought. I hope I don't have some kind of dweeb (her new word of the week). Well, her last one was smart too. "Oh." Susan said. Mark had wondered if she wasn't some kind of space cadet (his new phrase of the week). "Well, I guess that means you go there too. I'm sorry to say I've never seen you before. What's your major?" "Liberal Arts." Oh God, Mark thought. That was the major for space cadets. No matter, his thought continued, it's not like I'm really looking for brains right now anyway. Susan felt the conversation getting a little dry for her taste. "How'd you like to go to Papa's (the well-known pizza store on the corner of the University)? I could meet you there in about an hour." "O.K." Mark had answered feeling a little rushed. Susan had gotten off the phone already having in mind what she was going to wear. She had a special alluring outfit that she wore when she wanted a guy to want her before he could have her. She wore a hot pink tight-fitting, short-sleeve cashmere sweater with a very revealing V neck and a pair of the latest designer jeans that fit so tight you could almost see the bulge of her pubic hair. Mark was concerned about his outfit also. He knew this girl was a little fast by the fact that she had called him first. Where did she get his number anyway? Mark decided on his light, relaxed-fitting jeans and Oxford shirt. When Mark arrived at the pizza shop, he expected to have to wait for Susan for at least a half an hour (he knew females frequently played this game). Susan wanted Mark to know the importance she placed on time. She had already ordered a personal pan pizza for them to share and had picked the perfect booth for them to sit in. Mark was a little impressed on one hand and on the other was a little intimidated. He had never had a woman take so much charge of a situation outside of being in bed. Susan felt her nipples harden as he sat down in the booth. Mark couldn't believe his luck at meeting up with her so soon. "Well, I guess this is our formal introduction to each other." Mark said. "Yep. I hope you don't mind, I ordered a mushroom pizza ahead of time (she didn't know if he ate meat or not since vegetarianism was the new fad around town and almost everyone liked mushrooms)." Susan said. "Nah. I don't mind, mushrooms are my favorite." Mark said. Yes! Susan thought. She was trying to figure out if she wanted to play a good cat and mouse game but decided to go with the straight forward approach. She also didn't want him to think she did this with every man she met so she had to be smooth. "I've seen you around the school and didn't quite know how to approach you. I got your number from a friend of mine who happens to know 3 mutual friends of yours." Oh. Mark thought. "Well, you sure kept it a secret up 'til now. I wish I'd have seen you sooner, I would have tried to get your number first." Mark said. He used his sexiest, deepest voice for this conversation since he knew (at this point) where this relationship was going. Susan couldn't wait to get her hands on this guy but was still playing it as cool as her libido would let her. "That's a great shirt." I'd love to borrow it one day after getting up from the bed we just fucked in. Susan's thoughts were getting a little wild. They talked for hours about their likes and dislikes and their aspirations (though Susan really had none other than to be rich in any way she possibly saw fit). They left the pizza shop knowing the next meeting would be the climax of their newfound relationship.

Lisa and Tom

Lisa and Tom watched T.V. for about an hour and fell asleep soon after reminiscing for another hour. They both had to admit they had some pretty good times and they did surpass the amount of bad times. But, those bad times were very bad times and far outweighed the good times. Tom was still a little sore and really didn't have chasing Lisa on his mind. He had started thinking about his life in retrospect. At his age, he saw some things in his life he was disappointed about and some things he was proud of. Being that he had a failed marriage and no promising relationship on the horizon, he had frequent spells of loneliness and as a result never stayed home ending up in some woman's bed risking AIDS infection and God knows what else (even though he always doubled up on his rubbers when he had a doubt in his mind about the cleanliness of a woman). He talked to Lisa about this and felt closer to her at that moment than he had in all the years he was married to her. Lisa had the same feeling but not the urge to tell him her innermost feelings. Tom had confided in her almost every sexual encounter he had since they broke up during this revealing conversation. Lisa would have been super jealous a few months ago, but really sort of felt sorry for him. Tom had tried to replace the closeness of family life he had with her and Mark with sexual relations. He didn't know it at the time, but she had enlightened him to this fact during their intimate conversation. Tom, realizing his faults, started feeling dirty. He felt like a male prostitute and wanted to cry. Of course he didn't. He was letting go, but not that much. Lisa wanted to ask him if he had seen any black women but didn't. She and Tom only got on the black and white issue when they were arguing. Tom always "hit below the belt" during their arguments because he was always in a losing situation. He would say things like, "The only reason you're with me is because you can't deal with your own race. You don't love me or care about me. The only thing you care about is the fact that you think the mixture of us two could make a nice looking kid." This always infuriated Lisa. Only because it was partly true. When she was young, she could remember being with her cousin (who was more like her sister than her real blood sisters) and playing house. She would always choose to have a white husband with a big house and a kid with nice straight hair. Her cousin didn't want that (her mother always instilled the fact that she must value her black heritage and realize that she was an African Princess and her mother was the African Queen). She always said, "I don't know why you want some ol' stringy head baby, you can't even cornrow their hair." Lisa never cared about that because cornrowing was only used (in her opinion) to calm down the nappy hair that black people were cursed with. "Well at least I can leave it out without it looking wild." Lisa always replied. They would go on for hours. "Who said black people's hair looked wild?" Her cousin would ask and answer at the same time, "white people." Lisa's cousin had her mother's philosophy on life "down pat." Accordingly, Lisa's mother would attribute this behavior to her sister later when Lisa's feelings needed mending. Lisa would never talk this way with any other black person. She knew she was wrong, but somewhere down the line, the thought stayed in her head that white people were better and at least she could produce a half white kid if not a *totally* white kid. The ironic thing about it all is that that was part of her personality problem and she was seeing a therapist who was white. How was he going to help her? Tom had confided in Lisa the time he thought he had AIDS. Tom was on a wild weekend ride. He had sex with at least five different women from five different bar stops. That following Monday (as if he'd get symptoms that quick), he awoke to a bad reflection in the mirror (he had a mirror on his ceiling of course). He had a rash from his chest to his thighs (including the most precious part of his body). He had started coughing and thought he had seen an open sore on the tip of his penis. He called in sick and went to the nearest clinic (where he knew he wouldn't see anyone he knew or anyone he cared whether or not saw him there). He was given some ointment and cough medicine and sent home. Lisa laughed after this story. Tom was very upset at the time. "Yeah, I can laugh about it now, but then I was already thinking about drawing up my last will and testament." Lisa was hysterical at this time but realized that he was probably bearing his soul at the time and might not ever confide in her again. She couldn't have that happen. There was something she could never understand, but she always had to know Tom's innermost feelings and what he did after they split up. It gave her satisfaction knowing that he was never quite stable enough to make it on his own. For the first month or so, Tom was pretty satisfied with his wild lifestyle (or so he thought). When Tom and Lisa split up, Tom was disappointed and relieved at the same time. Lisa was just disappointed. She had tried going on dates (subconsciously getting back at Tom). But they were always dead end duds. Most of them were black and she was not used to their mentality and overall vibe.

Lisa

Actually, out of the 10 guys she met, 8 were pretty good catches, the other two were another story. One guy was struggling with the feminine side of himself and the other was married. Lisa's expectations of black men were that they were never professionals and they were only looking for women to take care of them. When the choices turned out to be that of doctors, lawyers, judges, and professional athletes, she was intimidated. Her friend, Cynthia, had set up these dates. Cynthia worked in a government building and knew most of the eligible bachelors. She always hated the fact that Lisa was married to a white man. She had purposely picked the cream of the crop so that Lisa could see what she was missing. Cynthia always felt Lisa had an identity problem and never quite knew how to make her fully aware of it. One time she tried being direct. "Listen girl, somewhere down the line you got brainwashed by those old sayings about pure as white snow and black cats being bad luck. White people are far from pure and black cats are nothing but black cats. Some like 'em and some don't." Lisa usually got defensive when Cynthia started talking this way. "What's the matter with preferring another race over your own? Aren't we all supposed to get along some way or another? That's why we have all these hate crimes and racist attacks." "Girl, some of those racist attacks happen because of what you are experiencing right now. Bi-racial relationships. If everybody just stuck by their brothers and sisters and stopped soaking up what the white man has put into our heads about the color black being associated with being bad, we would be a better people and nobody could stereotype us because we wouldn't allow it to happen. We would always protect our sisters and brothers. But no, we don't patronize each other, one sister doesn't like the other sister because she got more things or longer hair, we buy from Koreans and every other nationality but from our own. I'm not saying that this would happen overnight, but it's got to start somewhere. You think sisters are looking at you when you got that white man on your arm saying ooo, I wish I had that? No. They're saying damn, another sister sold out. Look, I'm not prejudiced, but I love to see a nice looking black man and a nice looking black woman together carrying on our heritage like it should be carried on. Yeah, I know we all may have a little white blood in us because of slavery days, but that's not happening now. We are not being forced to sleep with the white man. But now that we're not being forced we're doing it on our own. Like that's what we were taught to do. Don't you know we have to continue to love ourselves for what we are right now? This is not a black society, this is a white society (on top of that a white man's society) and until our race as a whole comes together, it will never be a black society or an equally balanced society for that matter." Cynthia was somewhat militant but only in the eyes of people like Lisa was she classified as such. "You need to calm down Cynthia. We aren't ever going to come together so why push it. Black people are confused and are ignorant to loving anyone but themselves (of course Lisa was talking about men in particular). Let's face it. Black people don't start up businesses, they wait for someone to hand it down to them. They'd rather work for some man (of course a white man) for the rest of his life and have nothing to show for it. At least I'm honest with myself. If I'm going to have a working stiff by my side, it's going to be a white working stiff. 'Cause at least I know he has the potential to move up just based on what he is and not what he knows (and she thought black men never really knew anything of importance)." "It sounds like you want to call us niggers like they do." "No, that word is still offensive to me too." "Oh, well at least you know you aren't the exception." 'Oh I know I'm black, but.." "But not proud,

right." "Well what's to be proud of?" "Girl, you all fucked up."
"No I'm not (feeling a little guilty)." Cynthia never really meant
any harm when speaking this way to Lisa but Lisa always left
these eye opening conversations, which was usually over lunch
dates, feeling lost and out of place. Somewhat apologetic,
Cynthia usually picked up the lunch tab. Lisa always tried to
forget these conversations before the next tongue lashing lunch
(they worked across the street from each other). The next time
they got together, Cynthia would always try being nice. She'd
ask Lisa questions that she knew Lisa was comfortable
answering. "Do you ever get people staring at you in a funny
way when you guys are together?" "Yes. But it doesn't bother
me. They just aren't used to seeing interracial couples." "Are
there places you can go where you don't feel uncomfortable?"
"Of course. There's this place called Justine's down on the south
side of town. There are inter racial couples from all walks of life
that come there just to have a good time. No one to make
derogatory remarks. Nothing." "I'm happy being who I am
Cynthia, but I just wish people would accept me this way also."
"Well, it's not that they don't accept you, it's that they

want to make sure you know the importance of trying to stay within your own race and that he's probably not looking at you as his wife, but rather his black wife. He's not blind and neither is anyone else." "Oh I know that, but I know he loves me for me not because I'm black." "But do you love him for him and not because he's white?" Lisa was relieved when a waiter interrupted them with the wine list. She did love him for him but if he was not white she wouldn't have given him a second glance. Cynthia played a major role in Lisa seeing Tom for what he was. A womanizer. The fact that he was white and made a good living always blinded her. Cynthia always suspected she had helped but Lisa never told her so.

Lisa was trying to get used to dating black men and dealing more with her culture. She had been talking a lot to her grandmother trying to find out about her history and reading up on the African tribe she was told her great great great grandfather had come from. It was a long road to recovery, but she was bound to see the light. She had stopped seeing her therapist and started seeing an herbalist who got her to stop eating meat and start taking vitamins and herbs for any and every ailment that she could possibly come up with. Cynthia was proud of her, but also thought she was going overboard. Cynthia was proud of being black, but never went the whole nine yards in finding out about her roots. Their racial conversations started changing to debates on whether people should name their children African names or not and whether people should wear their hair natural or permed. [Lisa had not yet come far enough to take the perm out of her hair.] But through it all, she still found Tom attractive. Was it because she knew him so well or the fact that regardless of whether he was black or white he was still a good looking man? Lisa couldn't answer that question. All she knew was that now she could look at him without being blinded by the fact that he was white and held a good job.

Cynthia

Cynthia knew she had changed Lisa's life in some way or another. She had told Lisa "One day you'll see what I'm talking about." Cynthia was a 35 year old single parent who loved black men, no matter what their fault. That was her problem. Cynthia had relationships that could fill a book. Her daughter was the result of her first love affair, ever.

Cynthia had been head over heels for her high school sweetheart. They had made plans together for the future eternity. They graduated, enrolled in college, got married, and had a baby (almost as quickly as it's written). Cynthia was scared to death when she missed her period. They were in the second semester of college and were both working at night in order to keep their little one room apartment. Her husband, Tyrone, had to quit school and work full time in order to get at least a one bedroom apartment and feed three mouths instead of two. The pressure finally got to them both and they split up after 1 year of their daughter's life, never fulfilling any of their future endeavors. Cynthia had seen him years later. He didn't look that good and she had heard that he was on drugs. Cynthia had basically gone from man to man looking for a replacement father and husband. She never found him. Her fifteen year old daughter resented her for having so many different men around and was your typical, rebellious teenager. Cynthia's rebound relationship after Tyrone was a guy she met on her job. He was handsome and had a promising future. He was a court stenographer and gave Cynthia the incentive to become one herself. All the girls in the office liked him (and had him she later found out) and Cynthia thought she was hot stuff when he asked her out on a date. Cynthia was a good looking woman. She had a smooth dark complexion and always kept her hair in place. Her figure was like an hour glass and she knew it. She made sure that whatever she wore accentuated her curves. They went to the movies and to dinner. He spoke so smoothly, they ended up at his apartment on the west side of town. Cynthia was swept up off her feet. He made good money and furnished his apartment reflecting that. He had all the conveniences of a bachelor. The black leather couch and black lacquered furniture along with the beige bear-skin rug in front of the working fireplace suggested nothing but seduction. As the conversation wore on, so did their longing for one another. Cynthia saw him getting hard while they spoke, but was more impressed that she could do this to a man without touching than anything else. He had poured some sweet tasting white wine for them both and it had made her very light-headed. Before she knew it, they were in his king size bed lavished in silk sheets. He was so good, it felt as if she was being made love to on all four sides. His body was big and muscular. His skin was so soft (she later saw vitamin E lotion bottles lined up in his bathroom and attributed his soft skin to this) she didn't know where the silk sheets started and his body ended. When he entered her, she thought she'd faint from ecstasy. He wasn't extremely big but if that man didn't know how to work that thing she didn't know who could (he turned out to be the best lover she had ever had). When they were through, she laid there breathless unable to speak. He turned over and went to sleep. Cynthia had already told her mother (who was taking care of her daughter) that she would be hanging out with her friend all night and not to expect her until the morning. She had called Lisa (she knew her from high school and was reacquainted again some years later after discovering they worked across the street from each other) and asked her if she could stay over her house just in case her date hadn't turned into an all night thing. She was in a deep sleep and was jarred awake by 3 horrible words..."You still here?" She had never felt so dirty in all her life. She quickly dressed as he rolled his eyes and opened the door for her to leave.

A co- worker made a comment to her that week when passing her desk, "Stung by the love bug, huh?" She was never humiliated like that ever again, she wouldn't allow it. After that experience, Cynthia delved herself into her work vowing to make herself the best court stenographer there ever were. She worked during the day and took a class during the night. She had made it as the most requested court stenographer in the office within 14 months. Dennis, the "love bug" was fired for fraternizing soon after his debauchery of Cynthia. After him, she only dated men with impressive professions (never anyone on her financial level or below). The next man she had gotten involved with was a lawyer who had been flirting with her ever since she was a clerk (Cynthia later achieved 25 years with her firm). He was not as good looking as Dennis, but hey, he was a lawyer. This relationship lasted a little longer. Three weeks to be exact. Cynthia had sex with him within one week. He was in no comparison whatsoever to Dennis when it came to the bed. But that didn't bother her so much. She started noticing how he would like her to do things a mother would do for a son. He would ask her to pick up his cleaning, wash up his dirty dishes on the weekends, and cut his food before serving it to him. That was not what Cynthia wanted. She finally told him what to do with his attitude when he asked her to wash his precious car (it was a Porsche). It was one weekend after seeing her accidently spill some soda on it. "You know you're going to wash my car, don't you?" "Wash your car?!" Cynthia screamed. "You must be out of your God damned mind. Your mother ain't here, your father ain't here and your maid ain't here. You need to get your shit together, my brother. See ya!" Cynthia had let him have it. She got in her beat up Toyota and sped off. She was proud of herself for initiating that break up. She later got an invite to his wedding. He married a white lawyer. She went on and on to one bad relationship after another. Cynthia was raised by her mother and grandmother. Southern women. They believed in old superstitions, home remedies and sticking with their own kinds of people. Black people. And even though no Crenshaw woman ever went into their old age with the same man they started with (most of their husbands, or common-law husbands ended up in jail or dead from not getting adequate health care), they stuck by their black men. Cynthia never looked at a white man in her whole life. Even though she never had a successful relationship, she still dated looking for that special black man.

Reunion

Cynthia and Lisa knew each other in high school. They weren't real good friends, just acquaintances. One day (a rare day since she were somewhat of a workaholic and rarely went out), Cynthia went to the corner deli to get a sandwich. It was just turning spring and she wanted to get some fresh air and a change of scenery. She caught the eye of her high school alumni and squinted in recognition. "Don't I know you?" Cynthia said (hoping she wasn't embarrassed by a "No"). "Cynthia?" "Yeah." "What's your name again?" "Lisa. Lisa Hand ..., I mean Lisa Johnson. It's Lisa Handly now though." "How are you?" Cynthia asked as if she needed to know. "I'm great (and she was at the time). I'm married now and have a son." "What!?" Exclaimed Cynthia (in high school, most girls in Cynthia's crowd thought Lisa would probably not bother with men and just be a career girl). "Well, I'm not married, unfortunately, but I do have a little girl." "What!?" Lisa had the same surprised response. (Lisa's crowd thought Cynthia's crowd was a bunch of sluts and they'd all ultimately have about five kids each.) They exchanged pleasantries and their job numbers. Cynthia needed a female friend in her life and found no harm in calling and inviting Lisa to lunch one day. Lisa was a little apprehensive at first, but Tom had been coming home late a lot and she was feeling a need for companionship as well. They had lunch and a few days later had dinner. It became an everyday thing which was good for Cynthia since her job often saw her working through lunch and now expected it. They became the best of friends. One night, Cynthia thought it would be fun to have her, her son and husband over her house for dinner. Boy was that a mistake. Cynthia never imagined that her newfound best friend was married to a white man. Lisa had never found the opportune moment to tell Cynthia, and didn't. Cynthia's daughter dreaded the night in the first place and when she met Mark, she thought she was going to die of buppiness. When Lisa rang the doorbell, there was a knot in her stomach. She knew Cynthia was not the kind of person to take her having a white husband lightly. She hadn't told Tom that she hadn't told Cynthia. Mark was not looking forward to the evening because he knew they (Cynthia and her daughter) were black and he knew his track record with black girls already. Cynthia yelled "Come on in!" Lisa immediately ran to the bathroom (her stomach couldn't take all the excitement). Before Cynthia turned the corner that separated her kitchen from her living room she was telling everyone to make themselves comfortable. When she rounded the corner and saw a white man on her couch (she hadn't seen Mark, he was looking at her Afrocentric pictures on the foyer walls), her immediate reaction was to scream. "Ah!!! Who are you, how did you get in here..." Lisa came running when she heard the commotion. "Relax. Relax. This is Tom." Lisa said. "Tom?" Cynthia asked trying not to sound disappointed. "Oh. Heh, heh. Nice to meet you. Would you like a drink? 'Cause I sure as hell need one (she mumbled). Uh, Lisa, could you help me in the kitchen please?" That was the start of their debate ridden friendship (although a good one). Lisa never felt the same again after that long talk in the kitchen. Tom and Mark were trying to make small talk with Shaniqua, Cynthia's daughter. Shaniqua was not responding. She constantly rolled her eyes and excused herself to call her girlfriend. Her mother had told her the phone was off limits for that night, but Shaniqua knew her mother was getting on Lisa for having a "cracker" husband. Finally, Shaniqua thought she'd make the best of the evening. Mark wasn't half bad looking, but he was still half white and that made him a dud in Shaniqua's book. Still, she offered to show him some of her new c.d.'s in her room. When they got there, Shaniqua asked Mark if he got high. "I used to, but now I'm on a health kick ya know." Mark tried to be as hip as he thought he could possibly get for this black girl. "Reefer's healthy. It's grown naturally, ya know." Shaniqua was being sarcastic, but Mark never caught on. She lit her joint anyway. Mark started feeling light headed not only from the smell, but from fear that her mother or his parents would walk in and catch her. "Aren't you scared your mom will catch you." "Oh, please. You better worry about my mother talking your mother into divorcing your father." Just then they heard

Lisa's raspy voice, "dinner's ready!" Shaniqua put out her joint and sprayed air freshener. "Well, let's go see if you're from a broken home." Shaniqua said. Mark couldn't believe the insensitivity of this girl. He knew black girls were rough, but this was ridiculous. Through dinner, Tom commented on how good the food was and things like, "Lisa, you need to take some soul food lessons from Cynthia." He thought this would ease some tension and make Cynthia feel good at the same time but it just insulted her (he didn't notice). She had cooked some smothered Turkey Wings with onions and carrots, some collard greens, white rice and dinner rolls. She hardly would have called this a "soul-food" meal. (Lisa thought that anything accompanied with collard greens was soul food. She hated when her mother cooked it. She thought only poor black families ate it.) Shaniqua had the munchies and never stopped eating long enough to say anything. Mark agreed with his father and answered periodic questions from Cynthia about school. Lisa, for the first time, was debating with herself about whether Tom was making racist remarks or not. Other than Tom's racist remarks, if he hadn't been white, Cynthia thought to herself that he could be a very charming man (but, of course, her upbringing would not let her think this consciously). They all felt relief when the (homemade) ice cream and cookie dessert was fully digested and it was almost time for them to be in their respective places. Lisa was disappointed. She really wanted Cynthia to like Tom and was almost as concerned that Mark had gotten along with Shaniqua. She ended the night by asking Cynthia to come to a company picnic that Tom's job was sponsoring and that there would plenty of people there (enabling Cynthia, or Shaniqua for that matter, to get away from what Cynthia thought was Lisa's "unacceptable" family if she wanted to).

Picnic or Outing

The picnic was fun. Both Cynthia and Shaniqua were surprised at how a different setting could change their minds. Cynthia had actually accepted Tom as a person she could come to like regardless of his color but she still was up in arms about his and Lisa's marriage. Shaniqua found herself being attracted to Mark and toned down some of her sarcasm. Lisa was pleased and couldn't hide her pleasure. During the course of a personality awakening day, Tom had to take Cynthia to the other side of the park to show her where the bathroom was. Lisa was busy mingling with the other wives of Tom's company, and, besides, she wanted them to be together as much as possible in her desperate attempt to make them like each other. More importantly, for Cynthia to understand why she married Tom. Cynthia was feeling pretty comfortable with Tom and didn't object to Tom showing her the way. Tom was, on the other hand, feeling attracted to Cynthia and couldn't wait to get her alone. When they got to the other side, they came upon the typical dark, damp bath house that smelled like 50 years of urine. "Go ahead. I'll meet you near the water fountain" Tom said. The fountain was on the other side of bathhouse and away from any busy traffic from the more-than-successful company picnic. "Okay." Cynthia replied, not thinking at all why he wanted to go way around the other side of the building to go back the other way. When she came out and went around the back, Tom made a remark that took her by surprise. "Took you long enough, babe." Her first thought was, what's it to ya and who the hell was he calling babe. She held back her surprise since she was feeling very amicable and didn't want to make waves right now. He put his arm around her and said, "You know you're very sexy." Cynthia couldn't believe her ears. Her first instinct would have normally been to slap him but she felt a tingle of excitement and let him continue. He grabbed her and kissed her passionately on the lips. He seemed corny to her (especially being white). Then she had a feeling of being bad, not a bad bad, but a kinky bad. This kind of relationship had been taboo to her all of her life and the thought of having a sexual relationship with this man brought the feeling of getting away with something that her mother didn't or couldn't catch her doing. She thought about Lisa and pushed him away but not before returning the passionate kiss. "What the hell do you think doing? Is that what you think about black women?" Little did she know that that's what he thought about all women. "I'm sorry." Tom said in his most sexual, please forgive me for being a bad boy voice: "Did I offend you?- I just thought you felt the same way I did." "Well, I di.., I mean well, I.." Cynthia didn't know what to say. She was curious but was also going against every principal rule she had ever devised out of all of her experiences with men (Thou shall not date white men). He kissed her again. Just then, Shaniqua was walking around the bath house towards them. She didn't realize who they were until she was up close (she was looking for a place to smoke her weed). "Oh shit!" She yelled. Cynthia nearly jumped out of her skin. Once Cynthia (and Shaniqua) got over the initial shock, she told Shaniqua to watch her mouth and tried desperately to tell her something that resembled the fact that he forced himself on her after a delayed, "get off of me!" to Tom. "So this is what my mother does. She raises me to believe that white men are hands off material and she goes behind my back and does just the opposite. Not to mention the fact that it's with your best friend's husband, much less anybody's husband!" "Niquie, let me try to explain this to you." "Don't bother, ma. I'm just glad my eyes are opened while I'm young." Shaniqua said as she ran away but just before she got out of their earshot, she said, "Don't worry, I won't tell." Tom's only (ignorant) reply was, "Whew, good thing she's pretty understanding." Cynthia looked at him and rolled her eyes. She couldn't believe her luck. She walked off and tried to avoid Tom the best she could for the rest of the trip. She was only thankful that she had driven her car and didn't have to ride back with them.

Cynthia had that day forever etched in her mind and avoided calling Lisa for a couple of days after that for fear of Tom picking up the phone. Lisa called one day and said, "Hey, you avoiding me or something? I tried calling you and I got your answering machine." "Oh, I was a little under the weather, girl. I think I caught something at the picnic." "Well, I'm glad you caught on to the fact that Tom is an alright guy." Cynthia didn't quite know how to take what Lisa had said so she kind of fumbled and said, "Yeah, well he's alright." "Don't sound so enthused." Lisa said sarcastically. Cynthia quickly tried to change the subject and they continued the conversation with idle chit chat. Weeks went by before Cynthia could bring herself to call Lisa at home instead of at work. She finally did and held her breath until Lisa picked up the phone. "Well, I'll be damned. Lisa never used profanity in front of anyone other than Cynthia. She felt it was something expected (stereotyped) of black women and chose not to do it. I don't

believe you're calling me at home." "Oh please." Cynthia
said. "Huh? ..., oh ..., Tom said hi, Cynthia." Shit! Cynthia
thought. Why did he have to be home? "Oh ..., tell him I
said hello." "Hello? Lisa said. Why so formal?" Cynthia had
once told Lisa how she always felt compelled to put on her
best manners and English pronunciations around white
people. "I don't know, anyway I called to ask if you wanted
to go to the movies. I'm feeling a little lonely and Shaniqua is
out with a friend for the weekend." "Well, Tom and I had
planned to go out for dinner and a movie ourselves..."
Cynthia heard Tom yell in the background, "Tell her to come
along, it'll be fun." "Hey, that's a good idea, come on Cyn, we
haven't been out for a long time." Cynthia didn't want to
seem like she was avoiding Tom so she reluctantly accepted
the offer.

Confrontation

Cynthia changed clothes about 3 times. She didn't want to
seem like she was dressing for Tom and she didn't want to
dress like she really cared. She decided to take a cab to the
restaurant because she knew she would definitely be drinking

tonight and didn't want to drive. Cynthia was the first to arrive at the restaurant. She was sitting at the table drinking out of a wine glass like she had an insatiable thirst. Cynthia was trying to ingest enough liquor in order not to be nervous in front of Lisa and Tom. Lisa and Tom arrived about 15 minutes after Cynthia was seated. Their eyes met and Cynthia waved them to the table. Lisa bent down to give Cynthia a hello kiss on the cheek. It had been raining and had become chilly so Lisa had on a raincoat. As Lisa turned to take her coat off, Tom bent down and gave Cynthia a very tender (almost wet) hello kiss on the cheek. Cynthia felt her face get hot. As dinner wore on, there were hot looks, touching under the table and sexual innuendos made by Tom. Lisa was never aware of any of these things. Cynthia excused herself from the table about 4 times before dessert was even served. She whispered to Lisa that she was probably getting her period and it wasn't unusual to keep going to the bathroom. It was pretty nasty weather by the time they got outside and on their way to the movie theater. Lisa was blinded from the weather by the love she was feeling. She was with the man she loved and the woman she had come to admire, respect and also love. Tom, being the gentleman he was, was sheltering his two beautiful black goddesses with his umbrella by holding them as close to him as possible. When they got to the car, Cynthia was relieved. She could get away by shrinking herself in the back seat of the car. But, to her surprise, Lisa immediately jumped in the back seat and explained to Cynthia that the rain stirs up her arthritis and she had to stretch her legs out before they cramp which could be very painful. Cynthia thought she was going to die. AS Tom began maneuvering the stick shift, he pretended to reach for the stick and "accidentally" put his hand on Cynthia's leg. "Oh man, I'm sorry. I didn't mean to do that." Cynthia just gave him a long hard look while getting out a pleasant, "Oh, that's O.K." When they got to the movie theater, it was still a half an hour too early for the next show so Tom got out and got their tickets while they waited in the car. Lisa couldn't wait for the opportunity for them to be alone. She wanted to catch up with Cynthia on what had been going on in their lives. "I never thought he'd leave." Lisa said. Yeah, me too, Cynthia thought. "So what's been goin' on, girl? You haven't told me anything about the new guys in your life lately." Lisa said this with almost the same boyish curiosity Tom's beloved friend, Bill, had used when asking Tom about his all too familiar weekends. "It's been quiet, chile." Lisa hated when Cynthia talked in that southern twang. It sounded "niggerish" to her. "I've been taking it easy and pampering myself." Of course, Cynthia couldn't tell her that Tom has been the only man on her mind and she couldn't shake it. "I hear you" replied Lisa. "Anyway, I've been trying to spend more time with Shaniqua. We've been having some problems lately and I've been putting them on the back burner. You know she's been smoking herb?" That was the term Cynthia had used since the 70's and wasn't sure "Miss Polly Pure Bread" knew what she meant, so she elaborated. "You know, pot." Lisa didn't want to tell Cynthia, but Mark had told her all about the night they had dinner at their house and how Shaniqua had offered it to him. "Oh no" was all Lisa could muster up. "Yeah, ain't that some shit." Cynthia replied in her best black lingo (which, of course, Lisa hated). Lisa saw Tom coming toward them from the theater. "Oh brother, here he comes." Lisa said. She had been feeling as though Tom was cheating on her and didn't quite know how to approach him. There was no evidence except for late nights at the job and the fact that every time she called the job, he wasn't there or was too busy to answer her call. He was also avoiding her in bed and when he didn't, he never climaxed right away (like a man who rarely had sex would do). She wanted desperately to tell Cynthia about it, but there was never an opportune moment lately. Not to mention the fact that she wanted to tell her without Cynthia bringing up the fact that Tom was white and saying I told you so (not that black men didn't cheat on their women, as far as Lisa was concerned, all black men cheated on their women at one time or another). "The girl said we could be seated in another 15 minutes." Tom entered the car saying. You guys want to go get some popcorn and other stuff? The line is probably very long and'll take about that long." This was another opportunity to talk to Cynthia. "Why don't you go get some stuff, we're having some girl talk." Lisa said. "Well, should I feel like a third wheel or what?" "Oh please, just go will ya?" "Alright." Tom said as he sighed and jumped back out of the car. "I think Tom's been fooling around." Lisa told Cynthia almost as soon as the car door slammed shut.

"What?!" Cynthia exclaimed knowing that he was more than capable. Lisa was surprised at Cynthia's reply. She was almost sure she would get a, I told you so. "Yeah, all the telltale signs are there and I don't quite know how to approach him." "Just ask him, girl. Don't you know by now if he's lying or not?" "Well, I think Tom's a very good liar and if he *is* fooling around he would surely put on his best bluff face." "Give him an ultimatum. Tell him you found something. Tell him anything you think he will believe in order for him to confess." Cynthia said. Cynthia wanted to tell Lisa that she thought Tom was no good, but she knew Lisa would only think she was saying this because he was white and was against the relationship in the first place. "I never learned how to be that conniving. There's an art to that stuff, you know." "Listen. You have to know for sure or you'll drive yourself crazy thinking about it." "I know. Well, we better get going. He should be pretty far up on line by now." They got out of the car and walked to the movie theater. Lisa felt good talking to Cynthia about Tom. Cynthia felt worse now than she did before they spoke. How could she betray her best friend? How could she keep this from her? Cynthia had heard of many situations where a best friend told another about her spouse's infidelities and ultimately destroyed the friendship they had before that. Cynthia valued her friendship with Lisa and didn't want to destroy it. She figured that if Tom was a dog, and he was, Lisa would find out soon enough and Cynthia would be spared the task of telling Lisa. The movie was long and boring. No one seemed to be paying much attention to it. Lisa was thinking about Tom. Tom was thinking about Cynthia and Cynthia was thinking about both of them and Shaniqua catching them behind the bath house. They left the theater not saying a word to one another. "Hey, wasn't that supposed to be a comedy?" Tom said hoping to break the silence. "Well it sure wasn't funny." Lisa said feeling a twinge of hatred for this man who was (or might be) taking advantage of her naiveté. They drove in silence. Tom politely opened the door for Cynthia when they got to her building. Cynthia said goodnight as she opened the door and stepped out. "I'll walk you up." Tom said as he leaned out of the driver's side window. "No. That's alright, the building is pretty safe." Cynthia had already closed the door behind her. "No place is safe these days." Tom replied. "Let him take you upstairs, Cyn. Better safe than sorry." Cynthia gave up and told Lisa she would call her tomorrow (facelessly answering the faceless question). When she and Tom got upstairs to her floor, Tom walked Cynthia to her door. "You know you didn't have to walk me up or to the door." "I know." Tom said. "Alright, you can go now." As Cynthia put the key in the door, she felt a flutter between her legs. "Now you know I can't let you go into your place without checking to see if anyone is lurking behind your door." Tom almost whispered in her ear, feeling like he was scoring points for each step closer to her bed. Cynthia opened her door and turned on the light in the foyer revealing the golden yellow walls. "See, no one there. You can go now." She wondered if Shaniqua was home. "Niquie?!, You home?!" No answer. Good, Tom thought. Damn, Cynthia thought knowing that she could have just acted like she was home for the sake of Tom not trying to push his way in. Tom was already on her heels and closed the door behind them. He used gentle but manly force to turn Cynthia around. He kissed her. She kissed him. Their tongues and lips became entwined, enclosed by their wet lips. Tom lifted Cynthia up against the wall. Her legs engulfed his thighs. She had on a spandex miniskirt that lifted easily. His pants were already unzipped. His hardness entered her as easily as he entered her apartment. BUZZ.... BUZZ. "Oh shit. That's Lisa." Cynthia said in a voice of ecstasy. "Wait..." Tom whispered as if someone could hear them. Cynthia pushed him off her as her feet hit the ground again and answered the bell. "Yeah?" "Did Tom leave? It's getting cold out here." Cynthia had to think of a quick answer. "Yeah. He's on his way down, I was looking for the sweater I borrowed from you. He's bringing it down." "Good, just in time. I'm freezing...I really hate this fall weather. I miss the summer already." Lisa said, never suspecting anything. Cynthia was reminded of the sweater when she saw it hanging on the hook behind the front door. She handed it to Tom as he was zipping up his pants. He grabbed her one last time and sucked her lips up into his. "I just want to eat you up." He again whispered in what Cynthia thought to be the most sexual voice she had ever heard. She felt her wetness at that moment and closed the door behind him. Cynthia took off her jacket and hung it up on the same hook Lisa's sweater was on. She walked through her living

room to the corridor leading to her bedroom. She felt
lightheaded. As she was passing Shaniqua's room, she
smelled marijuana. She knocked (from habit alone) and went
in. Shaniqua was smoking a joint with her headphones on.
"GET THE FUCK UP! WHAT THE HELL DO YOU THINK YOU'RE
DOING?" Cynthia walked over to a startled Shaniqua and
slapped the joint out of her mouth, "What is this, Niquie?
Why are you smoking this shit? Don't you know what it could
do to you? Who started you on this shit anyway? Cynthia's
questions were endless. She wasn't going to listen to
answers now anyway. She was too angry. Shaniqua kept
starting to answer her questions only to be cut off by the
next. "Well at least I don't go around kissing my best friend's
husband!" Shaniqua replied to Cynthia's horror. "Yeah, you
think I forgot or something?!" Whew. Cynthia thought. She
was glad she didn't walk in on them at the door. "Why didn't
you answer me when I walked in?!" Cynthia asked sternly
keeping her momentum. "I didn't feel like it!" Slap. Cynthia
whacked Shaniqua so hard her face turned red. Shaniqua
started crying. "I hate you!" Cynthia was slapped back by
Shaniqua's harsh words. She sat down next to her daughter

who had become such a stranger to her during these teen years. "How could you say that, Niquie?" Cynthia calmed down almost in tears herself.

'You don't care about me. So what I smoke weed? You never worried about me before. I feel like I'm all alone. You're never here and every time I try and call you at work or something, you say you're busy." Cynthia was stunned. Was all this rebellion her fault? How could she have been so blind as not to see her daughter hurting inside? "Baby, I never meant to ignore you or not be there for you. You should know that. I love you and never once denied that." "I know." "Well if you know that, why would you say things like that?" "I don't know." I just feel like you have more time for your work than you do for me." Cynthia felt as though she needed to pacify her daughter but also being the proud woman she was, she had to let her know the significance of all the hard work she was doing since the day Shaniqua was born. "You know, Niquie, there are things you have here that you would not have if I hadn't worked so hard all these years. When your father and I decided to split up, I knew that I had to do all that I could in order to live comfortably and for you not to want for anything. You may have gotten a little more than the average kid, but that's the way I wanted you to be brought up. You have to know that there's nothing in the world that I wouldn't do for you. I may have gotten caught up in my career a little more than I had planned and overlooked your need for attention, but you also have to understand that it wasn't because of a lack of love for you at all. Listen, I'm going to try and spend more time with you and make things better around here. Do you think you can manage to make the same effort?" "Yeah," was Shaniqua's reply. She didn't want to sound corny or like a little kid, but she wanted things to be better with her and her mother. "One condition." "What's that?" Cynthia asked with a frown on her face (she was expecting Shaniqua to ask something ridiculous). "Just don't start treating me like a little girl. I've grown up since you last looked you know." Shaniqua smiled after that. She was going to start being good, but that didn't mean giving up being a smart mouth completely. Cynthia replied with the same smile on her face, "Deal."

"What took you so long? It's freezing out here." Lisa had repeated to Tom as they pulled away from Cynthia's high-rise. "You know how you women are. You put something away and you can't find it for hours." Lisa took Tom's explanation smoothly. Tom's heart was beating fast but he knew Lisa wouldn't catch on to his lie. He was getting good at it. It never really took much. The other day, he took one of the secretaries in the office out to lunch and ended up taking her to a nearby motel. Lisa called the office all day looking for him. He had already told his secretary to tell all callers he had an afternoon appointment that might take the rest of the day. He and the secretary were very discrete. When Tom fooled around, no one ever really knew about it except for him and his best friend, Bill. When Tom got home that night, Lisa was waiting with an attitude that could kill. "What's wrong with you?" "You know what's wrong with me! Where have you been?" "Oh, come on babe. You know I had a late afternoon appointment. The client I had to deal with insisted on spending the rest of the day eating and going back to his office. He wanted to impress me with the office space he had just rented." Lisa fell for it as far as Tom was concerned. She had never really let these kinds of discussions linger very long. She didn't want to sound like a jealous wife. Although Tom thought she took his explanations well, she really never took the doubt out of her mind.

It Feels Right

When they awoke from their nap, they heard Nat King Cole's voice coming from Mark's room. "Unforgettable, that's what you are ...." Mark was singing to the top of his voice. Lisa and Tom, looked at each other with a smirk on their faces. "Must be a girl," they both said in unison. Mark always played Nat King Cole when he was seeing someone he was very interested in. Lisa went into the kitchen to find a late night snack. Tom went into Mark's room. "What's up, champ?" "Hey, dad." "New chick, huh?" "Well, yeah." Mark said with a smile on his face. "How far gone are you two?" Tom asked hoping to get something juicy. "Well we just dated once. We went out for Pizza. Dad?" "Yeah." "Conversation was hot." "Alright!" Tom Exclaimed while giving Mark a high-five. When's the next date?" "Next weekend. We both have finals this week and have to study so I thought it best we delay things in order for us to concentrate. Even though I won't be able to concentrate much just thinking about what's coming up this weekend." "Well, I hope you remember to where a raincoat." Tom advised ignorantly. "Come on dad, I'm old enough not to forget anything like that. Besides, this one's hot. There's no telling what kind of experience she has." "Those are the best kind. You sure you don't need any pointers?" "Now dad, give me a break." "Naw, man I'm serious. You know there's certain things that really drive women wild, if you know what I mean." "Dad, you don't have to tell me, okay?" Mark was embarrassed. "Alright, as long as you know." Tom hugged his son and said goodnight. "You know I'm very proud of you son." "Yeah, dad, I know." Mark was glad he had a loving father, but was also sick of him expressing it every time he thought Mark was "getting some." The week had passed and Mark could hardly stand the suspense of his upcoming date. Neither could Susan. They decided to go to the movies after a quick bite to eat. He drove to her house since she wasn't far from the university. Her house was a modest 1 family brick. The front lawn was only about 6x9 but well kept. Her mother obviously loved to plant as almost every inch of the lawn was covered with a carefully placed botanic wonder. They ended up getting pizza again. They went to see a new movie that had just come to the neighborhood theater. The movie was supposed to be hot and steamy. Susan knew that, that's why she suggested it. Mark hadn't heard much about it and really could care less what they saw. He just wanted to see her. The movie had several sexual climaxes and during each one, they seemed to sit closer to one another. Mark had gotten his arm around Susan and Susan had gotten her hand on his knee. When a love scene came on, Susan would rub Mark's thigh. Mark, not knowing what else to do, would gently rub her arm. At one point, Mark's head was pretty close to Susan's and when Susan went to turn around to ask him something (as if she didn't know) their mouths touched. They kissed passionately. Susan's hand ended up between his legs and Mark could hardly control himself. He pulled his free hand around to touch her breast. No sooner had they gotten to this point did the lights turn on. The movie was over and most of the theater was empty. Mark's face turned red. Susan giggled. They left. "Hey, let's go get some cappuccino from the coffee shop around the corner." Susan suggested. "Okay." Mark wanted to go to her house or somewhere private but would hardly push that issue. It was a Friday night and most everyone in town went home feeling tired from a long week's work. They were practically the only ones at the coffee shop when they arrived except for an old lady panhandler sitting in the corner mumbling to herself. They shared a booth. Susan decided to sit next to Mark instead of across from him. She had made up her mind that she wouldn't have sex with him until at least the third or fourth date. But, that wasn't going to stop her from having a little fun. They ordered their cappuccino and sipped slowly. "So how'd you like the movie?" Susan asked. "What movie?" Mark laughed. He turned around in his seat and took her face in his hands. "You are incredible, you know that?" "Oh yeah? Well you're not so bad yourself, honey." Susan said this as she clutched his penis. Mark was starting to feel pretty much at ease with her so he decided to lick her lips just before he gently kissed them. Susan's body went limp. Usually she contained herself just to make a guy feel inadequate. Mark was different. She felt wet between her legs and it felt good. She wanted to take him home to the confines of her bedroom (her mother never complained about Susan having boys in her room after the incident she had in junior high school), but she didn't want to come on too strong with this one. She wanted to keep him longer than the other sexual interests she had had previously (if he wasn't good in bed, she thought, he wouldn't be around that long either). Mark's hand slowly went up Susan's spandex skirt. He felt her wetness also. It felt good to him too. Susan moaned. Then she regained her consciousness. "No, baby, not here, not now. I want it to be special. Very special." Susan whispered. She turned around licked his lips and kissed him almost identical to the way he did her. Mark's hardness died down. He knew he was getting a little bold, but he had to go for it. "Okay, baby." He said. "Then I think you better go sit over there, 'cause I can't help myself." "I agree." Susan said as she moved over to the other side of the booth. They finished their cappuccino and talked for about an hour. They left the coffee shop feeling lightheaded. As they were leaving, the old panhandler called them nasty

teenagers. They laughed and practically ran out of the shop.
"You got me in trouble twice already tonight you know." "No
I didn't, you got yourself into trouble." Susan said as she
grabbed his hand and leaned her head on his arm. They
looked like the lovers of the year as they walked to Mark's
car. He drove her home and passionately kissed her
goodnight. She had almost invited him in when she
remembered what she had promised herself. But, their next
date was tomorrow night and she could hardly wait.

A Sticky Situation

After her heartfelt talk with Shaniqua, Cynthia was a little
sticky from her little escapade at the front door. She took off
her clothes and-took a shower. All the while thinking about
Tom. She couldn't believe what she had just done. Was this
her destiny, to love a white man? Love. She couldn't believe
she actually thought the word. She hadn't used it since she
was married to Tyrone. Hmph, I wonder what he's doing
now. She pondered. After drying off, she felt as if she
needed to hear Tom's voice. She called their house. Hoping,

contrary to previous calls, that she'd hear Tom's voice instead of Lisa's. "Hello?" She hung up. It was Lisa.

The Date

Mark was up early. He could hardly sleep thinking about his next date with Susan. He had planned a romantic date which should last the entire day. He called her and arranged for them to meet at the pier at which they would catch a boat to cruise down "Lover's Lane" (a strip of water owned by their town's resident billionaire lavished with fresh rose petals equipped with a tunnel lit with red candles). After their romantic ride, they were to go to the seafood district and have lunch at a romantic restaurant before going to see another movie. Susan was impressed by the fact that Mark knew how to make a full-day date without having to ask her what she wanted to do next. The day was beautiful. This guy was definitely not the love 'em and leave 'em type (of course she meant her loving them and her leaving them). She was sort of intimidated by this new feeling since most of the guys she went out with had no future with her and she never really cared about any of them. Mark was someone she didn't want to lose. She felt insecure with him. She had never felt this way before and couldn't tell whether she liked it or not. Susan's mother was out of town visiting her mother. [Susan hated her grandmother. She always seemed to know what Susan was up to. She never got away with anything around her and Susan hated that, she was used to getting her own way.] After the movie, Mark and Susan went back to her house. She told Mark to make himself comfortable while she made them something to drink. She blended up some Piña Colada's for them to drink. As Susan came back into the living room, she had a nervous feeling. She never felt this way before with a guy and she wondered if she was getting sick. Mark, on the other hand, was feeling quite great. He had a beautiful day with a beautiful girl and was hoping to have a beautiful night. They sipped their drinks slowly while watching a sitcom on TV. As the dash of Bacardi rum slowly entered Susan's bloodstream (she was never really a drinker), the nervousness turned into desire. "Come on." She said. "Where we going?" Said Mark. "Bring your drink up to my room." Susan said matter-of-factly. Mark quivered. He was in deep anticipation. They got to her room and Susan had a flash of dejavú as Mark sat at her desk. Her furniture hadn't changed much in the years that had passed since her favorite tutor was in that very same spot. Mark didn't want to seem like a young school boy by rushing things so he sat as far from the bed as possible knowing that he'd get there soon. Susan turned off the light. Mark's heart beat faster. She flicked on the TV. with the remote control as she flopped across her bed. Mark was a little relieved. He too was now starting to feel nervous, not that that would stop him from doing anything. "You can sit on the bed silly. I'm not going to bite you." Susan said softly. Her heart was beating also. They were, of course, playing a game. She knew their encounter wouldn't be long coming now. Mark replied. "And why not? I'm sweet enough." He heard that line on TV last week and felt glad to be able to use it. Susan thought it a little corny but was still increasingly becoming more and more excited. He walked over to the bed and sat down. He sat his drink on her night stand next to the bed and made himself comfortable by leaning his head up against the headboard. He pulled Susan back towards him so that he could put his arm around her shoulders. The TV was going but neither one of them could tell anyone, if they should ask, what was on. If anyone should look, they would see their shirts moving from the vibration of their hearts beating. Mark was tired of playing the game. He turned her head around and kissed her as if he were about to swallow a strawberry without eating the stem. Susan fell limp. They didn't rush. Their clothes were slowly taken off by each other and each part of their bodies explored as each article of clothing was removed revealing it. They made love for what seemed like forever and made love again. It was a new experience for them both. Susan never "made love" before and neither had Mark. They had both lost their virginity. It was late and they were exhausted. Susan put on Mark's shirt (as she had envisioned it from their first date) and went down to get a bite to eat. Mark turned the TV back on (not knowing when it went off in the first place). Knock, knock, knock. "Susan?" Marge asked as she opened the door to Susan's room. "I heard …"Mark was never so embarrassed in his whole life. He saw Susan's mother peep her white head around the door and immediately pulled the covers up over his chest. "Who the hell are you!?" Marge yelled. She had learned over the years that not every man in Susan's bed might be a stranger attempting to attack her daughter. Since it was dark with only the light of the TV, she hadn't noticed Mark's dark complexion. Susan heard her mother's yelp, put down their snack, and ran back upstairs. "What the hell is she doing home?" She mumbled to herself as she ran up the stairs. She pushed her mother aside as she saw what was happening. "Who the hell is this Susan? Get him out of this house right this instant! Do you hear me?!" "Don't have a heart attack mother." "Don't give me that crap. Goddamn it. Do it right now or you won't have a place to lay your head tonight." Marge said sternly. "Oh please mother. What are you doing home anyway?" "We'll discuss that later. Do what I said right now!" Marge turned around and slammed the door behind her. Mark was already half dressed by now and was headed towards the door. "Don't leave." Susan said. "Are you crazy? I've never been through this before and I don't intend to endure the wrath of your mother's mouth any more than I have to. Listen...he slowed down...I had a great time. I'll call you tomorrow." "Alright." Susan said feeling like her mother ruined her life in five seconds. Mark left and as he was walking through the front door, he heard Susan and her mother yelling at each other. Mark drove off thinking about what had just happened and frowned. Then he thought of the day and smiled. He felt happy. He couldn't believe his luck in love. It had never been so promising before. And Susan's mother, in all her fury, didn't mention the fact that he was black. Susan, on the other hand, had the worse fight with her mother she had ever had in her life. Marge had told her to move out and get her own apartment if she was going to act like a tramp and Susan told her that she would. Susan meant it. Marge was home because she had just had a fight with her mother and couldn't bear to stay with her another minute. Marge's fight with her mother started when she told her mother that she was going to sell the house and start a new life now that her husband was gone. Marge's mother felt as if Marge should keep the house for future grandchildren and stay in mourning for another 25 years like she did and never marry again. Marge ended up calling her mother an old maid and a spinster. Her mother told her to get out of her house if she was going to speak to her that way and Marge did. The next day, Susan called Mark. "Hey." She said as Mark answered the phone. Mark answered "Hey." "Look, I'm sorry about what happened last night." Susan apologized. "It's okay." Mark said. "The whole day couldn't be perfect." "Yeah. You're right. Well, anyway, it didn't end there. Me and my mother had a major blowout. She asked me to leave the house. I won't be able to see you today because I'm going apartment hunting." "Too bad." Mark said. "Well listen, I have to see you. Why don't I help and drive you around?" "Why didn't I think of that?" Susan asked. They hung up making plans to meet within the hour.

Hindsight is 20/20

Lisa hung up the phone. Tom asked her who it was before Lisa suspiciously told him that the person had hung up after hearing her voice. "Guess it was a wrong number." Tom rebutted. Yeah right. Lisa thought to herself. Cynthia had gone to bed that night feeling ashamed, confused and guilty for feeling excited about what had transpired that day with Tom. She didn't know how she was going to confront Lisa at

lunch the next day. Especially since Lisa had suspected Tom
was cheating and Cynthia could now confirm that suspicion.
Cynthia then started thinking realistically. I know Tom is a
dog. Could he have been screwing around at the same time
he was screwing her? They hadn't practiced safe sex.
"Damn!" she thought aloud, how could she have been so
stupid. Mental note, she thought -- get GYN checkup and stay
clear of Tom.

"Sorry Cynthia, we've been booked solid. My next
appointment isn't for another month." The receptionist at
Cynthia's gynecologist's office was familiar with Cynthia. She
frequented the office due to her many sexual partners (just to
be on the safe side). Her medicine cabinet was filled with a
vast array of birth control items (she had to fill a shoe box
with all the condoms she had accumulated from the generous
receptionist). "Well alright. I'll take what I can get. In the
meantime, can you send me some literature-on STD's and
AIDS?" "Sure. But aren't you educated on all that stuff?"
"Yeah, pretty much, but I only retained enough information in
order to look for signs of it, not the potential outcomes.

Anyway, I want to show the information to my daughter."
Good idea, she thought to herself. The receptionist
acknowledged her answer and verified her address. "Okay,
I'll send some pamphlets out today." "Thanks."

I Got a Lot on My Mind

"What's up?" Lisa asked Cynthia during lunch. "You look a
little spaced." "I'm alright. I just got a lot on my mind."
Cynthia couldn't tell her who but could tell her what. "Well,
what are friends for, girl. Pour your heart out." Lisa replied.
Then without waiting for a reply and sensing Cynthia's
hesitation, she continued. "What's the big deal? You've
never been so secretive before." Lisa, the guy's married."
Cynthia revealed in a shameful way. "Excuse me? Miss high
and mighty, self-righteous black woman?" "Alright, alright.
That's why I didn't want to say anything." "How could you
Cyn? Here I am thinking Tom's fooling around and feeling
miserable and some other poor woman is going through the
same suffering because of you." "I know Lisa. And I swore I
would never actually fall for a guy who was married but I

couldn't help myself. He's untouchable, he's like a candy shop and I'm the kid in the window being held back by it's parent."

"What the hell is that load of crap Cyn? Lisa was feeling as though she was confronting her own husband's mistress(es) (little did she know). "You probably threw yourself at this fool who was stupid enough to go for you and betray his wife. You know men will go for what's put in front of their faces and you put yourself there. You know Cyn, you really have come to a new low. I cannot believe it!" "But Lisa you know I wouldn't actually set out to date a married man!" "Bull! Lisa had started digging her heels into Cynthia. She was feeling the weight of her burden being lifted at Cynthia's expense. She knew Cynthia wasn't the blame for her husband's infidelities but it was starting to feel good not to finally have any built up emotion. She was facing them head on (her therapist would have been proud of her). Cynthia was getting pissed off at Lisa for relieving her tension on her (forgetting that Lisa was the victim here). "Damn you Cynthia, you really disappoint me. I thought I knew you better." "Well, goes to show you that black men are just as bad as white (she just said that for Cynthia's benefit even though they both knew she felt the opposite was more realistic)." "What?!" Cynthia exclaimed. It was getting late in the afternoon and most of the restaurant where they ate had cleared out. The people there (2 remaining tables of 3 people) were all in earshot and were trying to hear every word so as to tell their co workers about the juicy conversation they "happened to overhear" during lunch. "Look, I've told you time and time again, black men tend to be unfaithful quicker than white men. Black men always have something to prove." "To hell with that shit, you want to really know the truth? Do you really want to know the truth?" "What are you talking about now? You cannot argue your black self righteous stuff on me now Cyn. This one proves many of the points I've been trying to make as clear as day." "LISA, HE'S NOT BLACK, HE'S WHITE!" Cynthia couldn't help herself. At that moment, Lisa looked into Cynthia's eyes and knew. Cynthia's eyes were saying I'm so sorry it happened and motioned for Lisa's hand as she instantly knew what was going on. "How could you?" Lisa asked through water filled eyes. Worse yet, she thought, how could he? She got up from the table in a fury. She didn't go back to work. Cynthia sat there knowing what she had just done was inevitable but yet it also ended their friendship sooner than it had to. She cried and didn't stop crying for a long time. She called her office when she got home and through her sobs told them she had a family emergency out of town and would call them when she returned. After a couple of days, Shaniqua tried to comfort her mother asking what was wrong. Cynthia explained that she lost the best friend she ever had and told Shaniqua that no situation is worth losing a friend you know is a friend and would never do you wrong no matter how big the differences in your lives. Shaniqua understood only too well. She knew Lisa probably found out about Tom and her mother and couldn't find any sympathy for her mother. Just then, the phone rang. It was the receptionist from the doctor's office. "Cynthia, could you come into the office tomorrow at 3:15?" "Sure...What's up?" Cynthia asked curiously. "I don't know. He just wanted me to call you and book you." "Okay, done. See you tomorrow."

Goodbye

Lisa went to bed after throwing Tom's clothes out of the window. She was exhausted. All the emotions that ran through her during the day left her numb. There was nothing left to do but sleep. All she wanted to do was sleep.

Living Arrangements

It was raining and Mark and Susan had seen about six apartments. They were tired, hungry and wet from getting in and out of the car in the rain. "Listen. This is crazy. The ones you like are too expensive and the ones that aren't expensive, you don't like." Mark pulled over and added to his observances to Susan. "You know, I've been enjoying our time together and I'd like to make a proposition." Mark said this in a very serious tone which made Susan nervous. "Okay." She edged on for him to continue. "Shoot! Why don't we move in together?" He put his finger over her mouth while telling her she didn't have to answer until he heard him out. "I'm almost finished school and I've been thinking about accepting a job offer I got from a scout I met at the college job fair. I've been thinking about moving out from my mom's place and the dorm and I really love being with you. I know this seems a bit sudden, but we'll do it on a trial basis. If you can't take my idiosyncrasies, I'll help you look for a place again. No strings. Take your time to answer but right now I need to get a bite to eat and dry off." "I don't need any time, Mark, I'd love to live with you." "You sure?" Mark asked with the biggest smile she'd ever seen. "Yeah." They hugged, kissed and pulled off to go get something to eat. As Mark turned the corner, he was so excited he didn't see the school children crossing the street. He swerved and missed them as they all ran to safety on the sidewalk. As Susan and Mark's heads turned around to see them and sigh relief, an oil truck was in front of them about to back up. Before Mark could turn his head fully around and hear Susan warn him, Mark hit the truck head on. There was an explosion heard miles away. Mark, Susan and some of the children they had just missed were killed instantly. Just then, 15 miles from the scene, Lisa felt a nauseating curl in her stomach. She went on feeling this way until turning on the television. The announcer stopped his boring report on the failing economy and said, "This just in, a terrible explosion leaving six dead on Melbourne Place has left this community in shock..." The television blared as Lisa listened and looked in horror as she saw what was left of Mark's car. The telephone rang and rang and rang.

Reality Check

As her alarm blared and jarred her awake, Lisa realized that the phone wasn't ringing. It wasn't ringing at all. Lisa slapped the alarm off and turned over in bed. She lay there staring at her husband. Tyrone. "Ty?" She whispered. He replied with a grumble. She couldn't believe the dream she just had. She tried to wake Tyrone to tell him and after he turned over with his don't-bother-me scowl, she decided to keep the dream to herself. "Cynthia." She thought aloud. "I've got to call her and tell her about this one." As she picked up the phone, a mental note was readjusting itself to the front pages of her mind. She wanted to look up this dream in the dream book

she had just purchased. She walked into her modestly
decorated nine by nine living room and looked for the book.
She found it stuck between the cushions on their gabardine
couch. She opened it and realized she didn't know where to
begin. Lisa put the book down and returned to calling
Cynthia. She went into her galley kitchen and dialed from the
wall phone. "Wake up, girl! Have I got a dream for you!"
Cynthia hardly opened her eyes before telling Lisa she
couldn't possibly listen at that moment. She and Tom went to
an all night party and were just getting in the bed one hour
prior to her call. Cynthia told her she'd call her when she
awoke and hung up. Lisa couldn't possibly keep this dream to
herself. She had to tell someone. She walked toward her
son's room and looked in. His beautiful black skin on his back
faced her and she observed the deep rhythmic breathing of
sleep. "Mark?" "Damn," she said. "Isn't anyone awake
around here?" Just then the phone rang. Good. She thought,
maybe it's someone I can talk to. "Hello?" "Hey baaaaby."
the voice answered. "Oh, hi Bill," Lisa said disappointed.
"What do you want?" "Calling to talk to my main man, Ty."
"Well he's sleeping. "I'll tell him to call you."

Just as she was about to ceremoniously hang up the phone, she abruptly asked, "How's Marge?" "Oh, she's fine, baaaby. She and Susan going up to the clinic to make sure she don't bring no babies up in here." Ignorant mother f..., Cynthia thought to herself. "Well tell her I said hi." And she hung up without any further discussion. RRring. The telephone blared again. "Hello?" "Hey girl. I can't sleep. You got me curious about this dream. Tell me about it." "Well don't you know I dreamed Tyrone was your ex, Tom was my husband who cheated on me with you, and I was a prissy stuck up wanna be!?" "What?!, girl, you're sick." "Wait, it gets even crazier. After you cheated with Tom, you were about to find out whether or not he had given you the Aids virus. Then before all that Bill was killed in a car accident." "Wishful thinking, huh?" "You know it." "Well Marge had a whole new life and Susan was dating my son. Oh, did I mention that Bill, Marge and Susan were all white?" "Girl, what did you eat before going to bed last night?" "I don't know, but I do know that you were screwing every black man in America and had a holier than thou attitude. Remember that speech I gave you a while ago about keeping the black race alive?" "Yeah."

Cynthia painfully remembered. "Well you were giving it to me!" "And I had the nerve to cheat on you with Tom?," Cynthia asked without expecting a response. "Ain't that a blip?" Tom couldn't help overhearing that part. He turned over towards Cynthia and gave her a perplexed look. Cynthia answered the look, "Dream." Tom gave her an "oh, now I understand" look and turned back over. "I'll be back mom. I gotta run out to the library," Shaniqua peeked into her parent's room and announced. She was chocolate brown with straight hair Cynthia looked up from the telephone and answered, "okay." Cynthia loved her daughter and was very proud of her. She was glad she didn't have that typical mulatto look every mixed child seems to have. Cynthia was always in touch with her African American culture and surprised everyone when she fell in love with and married Tom while in the military right out of high school. Cynthia had felt a sense of no direction when leaving high school and felt the Army was the best thing to do after her mother warned her to either get a job or go to college. "Ain't no lazy ass gonna be sitting up in here while I'm on Social Security," she remarked one day. That was Cynthia's cue. She didn't

want to hear her mother complain for the rest of her life. As
Cynthia hung up the phone, she reflected back on Lisa's
dream. Lisa was glad she told Cynthia about the dream. She
knew the dream had specific connotations to their real life
and subtly wanted Cynthia to know that. Was Lisa serious or
did she find out what happened and was playing a mind game
on her? Cynthia thought back.

The Real Deal

After meeting Lisa for the first time since their acquaintance
in high school they became pretty good friends. When
Cynthia met Lisa's husband, Tyrone, her heart raced. She had
felt an automatic attraction to him. Tom was only her second
sexual partner and she hadn't had a lot of experience. She
believed this was the reason she had so many sexual
fantasies. Tyrone had felt the same attraction although
Cynthia didn't know it at the time. They bumped into each
other at a seminar one day. Tyrone's boss had insisted he go
in his place and Cynthia, being the workaholic she was, went
to every available business seminar she could find. "How are

you?" Cynthia asked obviously pleased to see him. "I'm doing great, how about yourself?" Tyrone replied returning the same pleasurable tone. They exchanged pleasantries and ate lunch together. "I'm sorry for staring so much," Tyrone said. "But I find you extremely attractive and don't quite know how to deal with it. If I'm offending you, please let me know. I won't say another word." "Unfortunately, I feel the same way." Cynthia replied. "I can't seem to shake this feeling and I've never felt this way before. I know that sounds corny, but I don't know how else to say it." Cynthia said. They didn't go back to the seminar that day. They went to a nearby motel. They made love into the night and both told their spouses they were booked into a hotel for the night so that they would return to the seminar the next day. They stayed in their room for the next day and continued to make love. Cynthia never fully believed her mixed marriage would last forever and often thought of it ending with her having an affair with a black man. They left the motel the next evening and never met up again. After she and Lisa became closer friends, she and Tyrone would never have eye contact for fear that someone might read their thoughts. Shortly after their brief interlude, Cynthia had discovered a sore on her vagina and immediately went to the clinic. Dr. Deluth explained that she had herpes and with this early detection along with early treatment, it could be treated fast and easy. During this time, she told Tom she was on her period (since he never seemed to remember her dates anyway) and after a week had gone by, she acted like she just wasn't in the mood. It was at the same time or soon after that Lisa confided in her that Tyrone was somewhat of a dog. He often slept around and it was common knowledge between them. She also said that she often slept around. Not because she was loose, but more because she felt it kept an even balance in their marriage. Lisa came from a family of no divorces. The women were abused verbally, mentally and sometimes physically. Never divorced. By any means necessary seemed to be their motto. Cynthia felt sick to her stomach after learning these facts and couldn't imagine anyone living like that. If she found out Tom was fooling around like that, she would end their marriage right on the spot. It would also be an easy out for her and she could live her life the way she really wanted...with a black man. Or better yet...black men.

When Tom met Lisa, he was not impressed. She was too crass and epitomized the stereotypical black woman. She called looking for Cynthia one night and he answered explaining that she was at a two day seminar. She laughed and joked at the possibility of Cynthia and Tyrone being together since Tyrone called and told her the same thing. She said, "why don't I come over and keep you company?" "No sense in us both being lonely." Tom tried to get out of it. "Well, Shaniqua is supposed to be home soon and I..." "NONSENSE!" Lisa said. "Shaniqua and Mark go to the same school, they're cramming for finals. All the students are pulling an all night study session. I'll be over in a half an hour." When she arrived, she stood in the doorway with a lovely raincoat. Nothing underneath. She bore a bottle of champagne and two champagne glasses. Tom stood with his mouth gaping at this cliché that only happened in movies. Lisa came in and gently undressed him. Tom was not a strong man. He didn't stop her. They had sex that lasted until dawn. Tom lay asleep as Lisa put her raincoat back on and returned home. When Tom awoke that day, he looked around and wept. He was sincerely sorry about what he had done. He cleaned the house thoroughly making sure there was no trace of Lisa and tried to wipe his mind clear of what had happened. He was sorry but not sorry enough to tell Cynthia a few days later. Tom too had found a funny mark on his penis and immediately went to the clinic. His doctor told him he had a sexually transmitted disease called Herpes and was given his prescriptions. Tom was relieved that Cynthia had her period and soon after didn't feel like being bothered. He had to make sure he was dormant before making love to her again. Tom always hated the get togethers they had with Lisa and Tyrone. Lisa constantly threw passes at Tom which made him very uneasy. Lisa knew about Cynthia and Tyrone. But no one, not even Tyrone, knew about Lisa and Tom.

Black Meets Black?

Tyrone and Lisa were invited to Cynthia and Tom's for dinner for the first time. They were all nervous but (subconsciously as with all parents) they made sure their children were there to take some of the focus off of each other's lives. Shaniqua and Mark were not as nervous as their parents. They already knew each other from school. Mark was part of the largest African American fraternity on campus. Shaniqua was part of the sorority only upper-classed (and unspokenly the "buppiest") blacks were allowed to be in. It was forbidden for any one of the members of these chapters to associate in any way. Mark and Shaniqua broke this forbidden law. On the same night of Lisa and Tom's infidelity, it happened. Mark was trying to make some extra money for a motorcycle he wanted and decided to tutor some students on calculus for a small fee. He had mostly white students and freshmen answer his ad on the student information bulletin board. The money came rolling in during finals week and he had pretty much made all the money he needed. The day before finals, Shaniqua realized she needed an A on her calc final if she wanted to keep her 3.7 GPA so she called a few tutors. They all told her they couldn't tutor her because they were all booked up. When she called Mark, he said he'd do it. Shaniqua and Mark met at the study hall next to the cafeteria. They had described themselves to each other in order to recognize each other. They studied into the night. Shaniqua knew most of the material and her tutor had soon turned into her opponent on a debate team. They first disagreed on calculus methods and then they (inevitably) got on the fraternity sorority thing. Shaniqua defended her sisters and he defended his brothers. Soon, they were the only ones left in the study hall other than some maintenance workers. Their arguments were heated and each had what the other secretly considered valid points. They neared the point where they were about to agree on the importance of strengthening the black male in a society that feared them through education and love. Then it happened. They gazed into each other's eyes and saw something past what they were representing. They saw, respectively, a man and a woman. Mark gently touched Shaniqua's cheek after lightly sweeping her hair back. He said, "you know you are quite beautiful." Shaniqua smiled. She would have sarcastically replied to any other guy by saying she knew she was beautiful. But being it was Mark and how they'd also argued about her sorority having their noses in the air, she didn't. Just as they were in the "kissing position," they heard someone clearing their throat. "Hem, hem." It was Susan. Susan was in the largest culturally sound African American sorority. These were Mark's fraternity sisters. They were on constant watch. Susan and Mark were like family. As a matter of fact, since their mothers were so close, they usually told people they were cousins. Susan and Mark often spoke of going to the same college during high school and had already chosen the chapters they wanted to pledge before choosing the college. Shaniqua and Susan's sororities were enemies. While Susan's sisters wore Afrocentric clothes, braided or natural hair and spoke of the upliftment of their race, Shaniqua's sorority sisters wore the latest designer apparel, got the best perms and cuts, and spoke of coming together with our white counterparts as one and becoming equals with them. When Susan walked into the study hall and saw Mark and Shaniqua, she felt her stomach curl with nausea. "My brother," she mustered. "Oh, em, Shaniqua, this is Susan, em, do you know each other?" Mark tried desperately to conjure an introduction. Shaniqua looked up at Susan and rolled her eyes. Susan replied, "My sister, you really do not have to resort to rolling your eyes. I know we have differences in opinion, but this chance encounter you are having with my cousin has nothing to do with our relationship. No, I don't appreciate the focus of your sorority and I know for a fact that you all have not a clue as to your identity or what your roots are. But let's call a spade a spade -- you do recognize a good looking black brother when you see one, but it won't be this one. Why don't you go back to running down your checklist of eligible light-skinned black professionals who have crossed over into neverblack, neverblack land." Susan tried to be diplomatic and sound like she wasn't threatened by Shaniqua. But in actuality, she was calling a spade a spade as well and she knew that if thrown Mark's way, be it light-skinned or dark, his probability of going for it was very high. Susan really wanted to take her by her permed and weaved hair and kick her ass. But, instead, she continued her speech. Look, we are a prejudiced society. It's bad enough we have white against black, but it's a damn shame we have light skin against dark skin. No, I don't like you and your sorority sisters, but it's not because of the way you look. It's what you stand for and the fact that you don't like us because we're not light-skinned. Although, it's all bull because you can sit here and try and seduce a dark-skinned brother and then later turn around and". "Hold on, hold on."

Shaniqua had to retaliate. "Listen, girlfriend . I am not your girlfriend, my sister." Susan quickly replied, "Yeah, and I'm not your sister." Shaniqua continued, "Anyway, no, me and my sisters don't wear African clothes," "Afrocentric either." Susan interrupted again. "Whatever! We also don't go around preaching to other black people to unite and get back to our roots. Some black people just won't unite and you can't make them see why they should. Furthermore, if you really want to get back to your roots, go back to Africa where you think your forefathers and mothers are from. Half of your sorority sisters don't know where they are descendants from or of. They could've been the result of some interracial marriage that may or may not have been strictly a black and white situation. They may be half Asian and half Indian born in a hot country. Who knows. But unless it's researched, don't be preaching to me about getting in touch with my African heritage." Shaniqua thought she really had let Susan have it with both barrels. "Look, Susan struck back, in this society, if your skin is not pearly white, you are a minority. Be it black, Spanish, West Indian or any other nationality. But 9 out of 10, when describing you, THEY will say you're black.

Period. And talking about going back to Africa. I personally wouldn't take my still westernized personality and impose it on my African counterparts. We, as a black people have to get ourselves together, right here in America before we think about trying to make our way back to the motherland. And be it interracial, or not, we all originate from a place that was one color. If you think that color was white, you got another thing coming. If we cannot agree on just that simple fact as a black race, of course there's going to be friction." Susan thought she was getting through to Shaniqua and then Shaniqua forged ahead with yet another statement. "But listen, if you cannot accept and love me for who I am, where do we start?" Then they stopped. Simultaneously they both realized Mark was gone. There was a note left on the table. "SISTER, IT'S TIME FOR A REALITY CHECK." Neither Susan nor Shaniqua knew to whom the note was written. When Mark got back to his room, he felt relieved and angry at the same time. Relieved that Susan got so high up on her horse she forgot about digging her heels into him. Angry because his "chance encounter," as Susan put it, was turning into something he wouldn't mind chancing. Susan grabbed the note and stormed out of the library and went to Mark's room.

"What's up?" Mark said as he opened the door. With note held high, Susan replied, "Reality Check? Was this for me or her?" Mark shook his head. "Come in, girl." Susan closed the door behind her. "Alright, Mark, let's talk." "About what?" "Well, you and me." "You and I," Mark corrected. "You and I have been friends for a long time." "Yeah." "Well, it's time I 'fess up." "What're you talking about, Sue?" Susan took Mark's hand in hers and told Mark she always loved Mark. There was a long pause after Susan decided to poor her heart out. "Well? Don't you have anything to say?" "Shit, Sue." "Why you decide to start trippin' on me now?" "Because, Mark. I've been lying to myself for a long time, but tonight when I saw you with Shaniqua, all my feelings came to a head." "There's a word for that Sue, its called jealousy." "No, Mark, that's not what it is at all. You've gone out with other good looking girls before and it never bothered me as much as it's bothering me with Shaniqua." "Why?" Mark asked sincerely. "Because. There's something there. There's something that could actually develop between you two. There's an attraction that I never saw with any other girl and you." "That's not entirely true, Sue." "I definitely love you and have always been attracted to you." "What?" Susan felt cheated. "Well, you have always made sure you referred to me as your cousin to all your friends and mine. You always made sure I knew you felt like a sister to me, never more." "So?" "So, I didn't push it." "But, you're right Susan, I feel attracted to Shaniqua more than any other girl. You know why?" "Why?" "Because I finally gave up on you."

RRRING! The telephone blared. Mark answered, "Hello?" "Reality Check?" Shaniqua was asking on the other end. Mark squirmed. "Yeah, well, um, could I call you back? I'm in the middle of something right now." Mark spoke softly and Susan knew right away it was a female. She knew him more than any sister or cousin could. "I promise I'll call you before you go to bed. Mark was almost silky. Susan used it as an exit sign. Just as she turned her heel, Mark grabbed her arm. He hung up the phone and continued his smoothness. "Don't go." When Shaniqua got back home, she thought about Mark, Susan and the note. Was he referring to her? If he was, he was probably right. She couldn't believe what had come out of her mouth. Go back to Africa? What was she thinking? Her mind turned to how her and Mark's conversation was getting hot and heavy before Miss Kunte Kinte came in the room. Damn, that bitch. Well, I'm definitely not letting him get through my fingers. She called him right away. His number still fresh in her memory. "Reality Check? I hope the note was for Susan...between something?" She was just as smooth as Mark. "You better promise to call me back. Alright, bye." Shaniqua couldn't wait for the next interlude. She lay on her bed and fell asleep thinking about Mark. RRRING! Shaniqua's hand was still on the phone when the phone rang. Before she realized that it was the next morning and Mark hadn't called her back the night before, her mother was cheerfully greeting her. "Good morning honey, I just got back from my seminar." Cynthia was still light-headed from her interlude and needed to hear her daughter's voice to overcome (a little) guilt. Shaniqua couldn't imagine anyone else calling but Mark because no one knew she was staying in her friend's dorm room but him. "How'd you know how to reach me?" "You know when I want to find my girl, there's never a problem." "You called

Lisa, didn't you?" "Yes, and she called her son and the rest is history." "Well anyway, glad to hear from you so soon. When'd you get back?" Shaniqua asked cheerfully. "I just walked in the door. I wanted to ask you to clear your calendar for May 13th." "Why, what's up?" Cynthia had a brainstorm on her way back from the seminar. She wanted to organize a dinner party for all her closest friends and their children. The thought of being uncomfortable in front of Tyrone hadn't yet hit her. "I'm having a dinner party to celebrate the end of finals and your upcoming graduation." "Oh, that sounds nice. Consider my calendar clear. But aren't you being a little premature? That's two months away. "Well, there's no good time like the present. Anyway, it's about time all my good friends got together in one place to have a good time." "Alright, well I gotta get back to the books, I have a calculus test in an hour and need some last minute cramming." "Okay, sweetheart, I'll talk to you later." Shaniqua wanted to also keep the line free just in case Mark called.

RRRING! Mark answered the phone. "Hello." "Hey, honey, its mom. Listen, I didn't mean to wake you up but do you know where Shaniqua is right now?" "Oh, um, yeah, she's at 555 6698." "Okay, thanks, I'll talk to you later." Lisa hung up before Mark could ask why she wanted to know. Mark looked over at Susan sleeping peacefully. He regretted what had happened the night before almost immediately. After grabbing Susan's arm to stay with him, he realized his mistake. It was too late, he thought. The look Susan gave him was one that said "I love you and you love me, so why not?" Mark couldn't possible reject that look. It would have hurt her too much. As he made passionate love to Susan, he only thought of Shaniqua. There was no mistaking that fact. He knew he really wanted to be with Shaniqua, but felt an obligation to Susan. He looked down at the marks on his arm left by Susan's braids and the reality of what he had done hit him hard. He threw on his jeans and a t shirt and left Susan sleeping. Mark anxiously knocked on Shaniqua's door. He suddenly felt there was no time to waste. Shaniqua opened the door and was pleasantly surprised. "Well, I guess a personal visit is better than a phone call anytime." "Listen, I

just wanted to let you know how I feel about you." "Go
ahead" Shaniqua anxiously waited to hear as well as see
Mark's lips say something that would inevitably make her
melt. "I like you...I like you a lot." Suddenly, Mark felt like a
schoolboy talking to a girl for the first time. He couldn't tell
her about Susan just yet, but he could tell her what his
feelings were. She looked at him and her eyes made him feel
just as his lips had made her feel by uttering those simple
words. He thought, there goes that look again. They kissed.
Mark felt so right, as did Shaniqua. Mark gently walked her to
the twin size dorm bed that was still made up since she had
fallen asleep on top of the hot pink bedspread. She knew
now was neither the time nor the place. Her friend who
stayed in the dorm room was due back any minute and she
knew that the wait would intensify their feelings for each
other. As she pushed him up from on top of her and sat up,
she whispered, "Stop." "What's wrong?" Mark answered
with disappointment. "Not here." "Why not? I want you
now." He said this brushing her hair to the side to reveal her
soft brown eyes. Shaniqua was just as anxious as Mark was,
but just then, a key opened the door. It was Shaniqua's

friend. "What's up?" she asked. "Nothing much," Shaniqua
said as she conspicuously eyed Mark. "Should I come
back?" Shaniqua's friend asked just as conspicuously. No,
I'm just about to leave. Besides, my test is soon to start."
Thanks for letting me use your room, I'll call you later."
Okay, see you later." Shaniqua picked up her books with
one hand and pulled Mark along by his hand with the other
like a mother pulling her young child from a bad situation.
Cynthia had gotten in touch with everyone. Bill and Marge,
Tyrone and Lisa. Lisa thought about the dinner party and
got excited. She knew she would make Tom uncomfortable
and she also wanted to see if there were any tell
tale signs that Cyn and Tyrone had an affair. She knew it
would break her heart to see that it was true, but she had to
know. Lisa could always tell when Tyrone was in the
presence of a woman he slept with. It has happened more
times than she had cared to remember. The first time it
happened turned into a fiasco.

They had gone to an office party together. As they sat
around the conference room filled with food and liquor, she
kept noticing a woman trying to check her out with her

peripheral vision. At first she thought that maybe it was a bitch thing. But then she noticed Tyrone trying to avoid her and avoid introducing her. Finally, one of the loud mouthed secretaries (probably wanting something to add to the office gossip the next day) pulled the chick over to introduce her to Lisa. There was such uneasiness, his colleagues that didn't know, now knew. Lisa's immediate reaction was to slap him. WHACK! "You mother fucker! She stormed out of the conference room and took the car home. They had a big fight that night where Tyrone tried consistently to deny everything. He later admitted it and apologized profusely. That was the first time she knew she would never be bothered by Tyrone's infidelities again. Lisa wondered how someone so bad at lying could have the nerve to cheat. All she knew was that she never really had the nerve to cheat on anyone but she was a hell of a better liar than Tyrone. This time was different. She felt a friendship developing with Cynthia and never dealt with Tyrone messing with one of her friends. It was a week after Cynthia called with her special invite before Lisa told Mark about it. Mark was all gamed to go. He had told Shaniqua that it would be fun to get together like a couple getting ready to get married and go to the engagement dinner. Mark never thought about Susan and her family being there as well. Mark never really found the right way to tell Susan they had made a mistake so he was trying to play his cards right. Mark could not even believe how he had handled things. Susan was convinced she had beat Shaniqua. Shaniqua was convinced that Susan was well aware that Mark clearly chose her over Susan. Mark had mentioned his dilemma to his father. Of course Tyrone had the upcoming dinner to think about. He was very nervous about coming face to face with Cynthia. He knew Lisa would pick up his nervousness. His only advice to Mark was to "be honest." Mark replied with a question, "have you always been honest with mom?" Tyrone whipped his head around as if Mark had found out his horrible secret. "Why do you ask?" "I don't know. I just think that in all the time you guys have been together that you must have bent the truth just a little, right?" "Well, maybe a little." Tyrone replied. The conversation was interrupted with the phone ringing. It was Susan for Mark. Mark told his father to say he wasn't there. The phone rang five minutes later. It was Shaniqua. Mark had no lies (other than about Susan) for her. Even though their parents were friends, it was odd that they never really met. Whenever his mother would talk about her friends, Mark would instinctively tune out. Truth be told, Lisa often tried to have Mark and Shaniqua introduced but Mark would always conveniently not be home. Susan never really showed interest in Mark when they all got together so she never bothered playing cupid. "Hey, girl what's up?" "Oh nothing. I just wanted to ask if your mom told you about the dinner my mom's having on May 13." "Um, yeah." "I'll definitely be there." I told you, I like the idea of us getting together like that. It's very pre-wedding sounding. "Hmm." Shaniqua muttered at his preoccupation with the assumption of such a serious commitment like marriage. Shaniqua really liked Mark, but certainly was not ready for marriage. Mark only knew how good he had felt with Shaniqua and thought she felt the same way. Mark thought that if he threw the word marriage around that Shaniqua would feel more comfortable letting her guard down. He always felt that once a man said or even uttered the word that it showed how committed the man was willing to be. The dinner idea was not really thought long and hard about by Cynthia before inviting everyone. She hadn't given any thought to the uncomfortable feeling she (and Tyrone) might have. After all the arrangements had been made (she hired a caterer and a florist for the affair), she realized what a mistake she may have made. The time was drawing near and so was her fear of the inevitable. She had come to know Lisa pretty well. Lisa was the most insightful and perceptive person she knew. She couldn't bear looking in her eyes while Tyrone was near. It was a catch-22 situation. If she looked at Lisa, she would immediately know something was going on. If she didn't, that would be a dead giveaway as well. She decided to make it a little easier on herself. She called the catering place and told them she would serve everything herself. This would at least keep her busy enough not to seem preoccupied with avoiding Tyrone's nervousness and Lisa's perception. She was also awaiting Cynthia's dinner with bated breath. After Susan and Mark had made love, she couldn't sleep. She knew that their relationship was now changed forever. She didn't mean for it to turn out the way it did, but her jealousy had gotten the best of her. She had to beat Shaniqua at all costs. When

Mark got up to answer the phone that morning, Susan pretended to be asleep. She waited for Mark to leave the room and called her friend. "Frat sisters 'till the end" was the end of the conversation. Of course, the information that was returned to Susan was vital to how she would act at Cynthia's dinner. When Marge told Bill about the dinner, Bill lit up. "You know your girl got a thing for me, right?" "What are you talking about Bill? Marge asked as if he had lost all his faculties. "Cynthia digs me." "Bill, why would you even think such a thing? Do you have a thing for her?" "Naw, baby. You know I only have eyes for you. Now come over here and give me some lovin'" "Fuck you Bill!" "Yeah, that's right come on over here." Bill replied as if it was an invitation. They had a five minute sex break and as usual, Bill felt manly and Marge felt used but satisfied. Marge, of course, didn't know it, but Bill had his mind on Cynthia during the entire five minutes. Bill didn't know it, but Marge was thinking about what to cook for dinner. They both looked forward to the dinner. Tom had his own agenda for the dinner. He knew Lisa would be throwing passes at him and he refused to succumb to her will to make him nervous. He was feeling a strength lately that would be perceived, had he been a woman, as having P.M.S. He couldn't wait for the opportunity to tell his shithead of a friend to stop hitting on his wife. He was equally anxious to let Lisa know he wasn't afraid of her. The day had come. There was an air of relief because the finals were over and Mark, Shaniqua and Susan were all fully aware they had passed and were graduating in June. Cynthia was kicking herself more and more as the day drew near to her unthought-of dinner. The caterer had called one day when Lisa was visiting her having one of their heart to hearts about life. Cynthia was in the bathroom when the phone rang. When she emerged from the bathroom, Lisa told her that the caterer had called to let her know that the serving would be free with the amount of food she ordered so the only natural thing to do was for Lisa to okay it. Cynthia's body twitched as if a spider had crawled up her back. But now it was too late. The caterers arrived on time about one hour prior to the dinner. Cynthia laid out place cards trying very strategically to place everyone just right. Of course the first thing was for her not to be directly across from Lisa or Tyrone. She placed Bill and Marge across from them with their respective children opposite each other. She placed herself and Tom on either ends of the table with Shaniqua on the same end as Mark, Susan and Tom. Shaniqua had been in her room during all the preparation. Typical, but glad she is out of the way is what Cynthia thought. But when she materialized at the smell of the gourmet aroma, she noticed the place cards. She really hadn't mentioned her and Mark's relationship to Cynthia in detail. Detail meaning she hadn't really mentioned the name of the new guy she was seeing that made her feel so good. She knew Cynthia would get all mushy and stuff and make a big deal and she didn't want to deal with that. When she saw she was sitting next to Susan, she nearly had a temper tantrum. "Mom! What's this?!" "What's what, hon?" Cynthia came out of the kitchen licking her fingers to see Shaniqua holding the place card in her hand. "Oh that." "I thought it would be nice for all you kids to be at the same end of the table. You will have a lot more in common than some of the adults." Cynthia didn't seem to notice the anger rising in Shaniqua. "I don't want to sit next to this fake African." Cynthia returned the nasty remark with a look of displeasure. "Well she is." Shaniqua answered. "Put me over there next

to you." Cynthia had other things to worry about and just
gave up the argument and told Shaniqua to do whatever she
wanted. Tom was also staying out of the way when the
sound of his own stomach awoke him from his nap. He came
out to the kitchen (not noticing the place cards at the table)
to see what he could pick on before the festivities began.
Cynthia politely slapped his hand and the white gay server
peered over his nose. The fresh fruit and flowers gave the
house a lovely aromatic smell and with the light Spring breeze
coming through the window, everything was perfect. The
first to arrive was Bill and Marge. Susan had told them to go
on ahead of her so that she could make a grand entrance.
They came in making small talk while Bill made some crack
about how good Cynthia looked with her shimmering
stockings. "Hey, are those stockings or panty hose?" "Them
there stockings is some sexy shit." "Why don't you shut up,
Bill." Marge said feeling embarrassed as ever. "Whatever."
Cynthia managed to come back with. "Hey, you mind if I light
up this cigar?" "Yeah, go out on the terrace." Cynthia
answered. Tom just sneered at him and joined him on the
terrace. Cynthia had only hoped that Tom kept him out there

until dinner started so she didn't have to deal with him.

Lisa, Tyrone and Mark arrived next. As usual, Cynthia was very happy to see Lisa and greeted Tyrone and Mark almost diplomatically. "Where's Niquie?" Cynthia was a little surprised at Mark asking for her daughter by her pet name. "She's in her room listening to some of that loud music you guys listen to." "Do you mind if I go back to see her?" "No, go ahead. Maybe you can get her out of that room long enough to say hello to everyone." Tyrone joined Tom and Bill on the terrace and talked as much guy talk as he could muster. His mind was preoccupied, but he couldn't let on that it was. Knowing Bill, he'd say, "You act like you having an affair with one of these fine women up in here or something." And he would be right. So the best thing to do is to keep Bill talking about himself or what he could do and no one had to really say much else. Lisa sat down with Marge on the couch and had a glass of wine. She always knew exactly where the liquor was in everyone's house. They had idle chit chat and laughed about Bill's rudeness. So far so good is what Cynthia was thinking. Mark was so preoccupied with getting to see Shaniqua that he didn't even notice Marge and Bill were there. If he had, he would have thought of the possibility of Susan coming. "Your ex out there?" Shaniqua asked. "What are you talking about?" "Susan." "Why would Susan be here? Don't tell me they're here too?" "Well, I'm sure if Susan were here, she'd be hanging all over you by now, so I guess she's not here." Shaniqua said. "Well she's not. So whatcha doing?" "Nothing." Mark moved closer to Shaniqua and grabbed her hands to pull her off her bed. He moved her closer to him and asked, "Whatcha wanna be doin?" She kissed him passionately and said, "Eating. I'm starving." "You know you put such a hurtin' on me sometimes." She pulled his hand out of the room as they proceeded to join the others.

THE END

###

Contact the Author

Thank you for reading "Reality Check, Does Race Define a Relationship." I hope you enjoyed it! Please look for other titles from this author in the near future. Please leave a personal review by emailing mattersincorporated@gmail.com and/or leave a review of this book with your favorite retailer.

Hey, why not "Like" my Facebook page at https://www.facebook.com/MATTERSEntertainment